The
Gardener's
Guide
to Cactus

THE PLENTIFUL
RIPE FRUIT ON THIS
ENGELMANN'S
PRICKLY PEAR IS
READY FOR HARVEST.

— The Gardener's Guide *to* —

Cactus

The 100 Best Paddles, Barrels, Columns, and Globes

SCOTT CALHOUN

TIMBER PRESS

PORTLAND – LONDON

All photos by the author except: photos on pages 59 and 95 used with permission of Lauren Springer Ogden; photos on pages 44 and 121 used with permission of Greg Starr.

Designed by Michael Pangilinan and Kristin Eddington

Published in 2012 by Timber Press, Inc.

The Haseltine Building
133 S.W. Second Avenue, Suite 450
Portland, Oregon 97204-3527
timberpress.com

2 The Quadrant
135 Salusbury Road
London NW6 6RJ
timberpress.co.uk

Printed in China

Library of Congress
Cataloging-in-Publication Data

Calhoun, Scott.

The gardener's guide to cactus:
the 100 best paddles, barrels, columns,
and globes/Scott Calhoun.—1st ed.

p. cm.

Includes bibliographical references and index.

ISBN 978-1-60469-200-6

1. Cactus. 2. Gardening. I. Title.

SB438.C325 2012
583'.56—dc23
2011025181

A catalog record for this book is also available from the British Library.

To my dad, who introduced me to the desert and taught me how to remove cholla cactus spines from my leg with a comb.

HOT PINK AND HIGHLY PERFUMED, THE BEEHIVE CACTUS FLOWERS MAKE IT AN IRRESISTIBLE GARDEN ADDITION.

Contents

Preface

When it comes to garden plants, cactus are anything but standard issue.
The bulk of home gardens contain exactly zero species of cactus; perversely, being thus overlooked makes them one of the most enticing plant families for those hoping to veer from the mundane toward the sharp side of gardening. However, if your first thought about growing cactus is "ouch"—this book is designed to get you past that. Imagine cactus flowers heavily scented of honey and chocolate; a hedgehog species with fruit that tastes like strawberries; and a lumpy, thornless, lime-green column whose skin feels like melted wax. If you think of cactus solely as plants confined to rock-strewn deserts, you might be pleasantly surprised to discover that several species grow in the steppe climate of the short-grass prairie, happily sidling up to grama grasses.

I have always admired cactus for their anthropomorphic qualities. They have spines, we have spines, and like us, many species have bodies, joints, and even ear- and arm-like appendages. More than twenty years ago, when I began designing my first garden, I considered the members of the cactus family solely as accent plants—to be used here and there as curiosities, but rarely more than that. Oh, how my perspective has shifted!

Over time, cactus and their succulent cousins have moved to the center of my garden design universe. In gardens, cactus stand as living sculptures that get more and more interesting as they mature over the decades. They form the prickly heart of some of the most interesting gardens in the world. Designs peppered with cactus have become my new design paradigm. To boot, these designs are of the very most water-thrifty and undemanding sort. Especially in terms of water, cactus ask little of their keepers. I started substituting cactus in place of thirsty and finicky perennials, seeking out the most garden-worthy specimens—plants with red spines, thatches of needles, and brightly colored flesh. The longer I kept cactus, the more I appreciated them; they are exceptionally venerable plants. Many species are so long-lived that prized plants can be passed down from one generation to the next.

As I explored the many excellent field guides and technical botanical tracts that treat the cactus family, it occurred to me that the literature remarked little about the garden-worthy attributes of the plants in the family. I became convinced that the aesthetic and sensory qualities of the family were due more exploration. That conviction is the genesis for this book.

In the pages that follow, I feature one hundred of the most interesting and versatile North American cactus species. As with all such lists, this one is to some degree arbitrary; the choice of species is based on my tastes as a garden designer and plantsman, and with an emphasis on fitting them into a garden setting. In that spirit, all of the cactus are sorted by shape first rather than a simple A to Z list by botanical name alone. They are grouped as follows: low and mounding, barrels and globes, paddles and rods, and columns. In addition to the horticultural information you'd expect to find in a book like this, I'm adding an entry for each species with design suggestions that in some cases include companion plants. It is possible that my enthusiasm for these endlessly fascinating plants will be contagious as you browse this book. I aim to get you hooked—hopefully not literally.

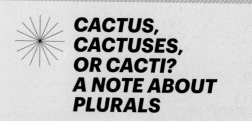

CACTUS, CACTUSES, OR CACTI? A NOTE ABOUT PLURALS

► What to call more than one cactus is a decision anyone writing about this spiny plant family has to address. Unfortunately, there is no one right answer; there are three acceptable ways to refer to cactus in the plural: cacti, cactuses, or cactus. In this book, I have chosen to steer away from the more scientifically and technically correct term "cacti" and the awkward "cactuses" in favor of the easy and plain "cactus." My intent is to bring new gardeners into the prickly plant fold and I'm hoping that simply using "cactus" to refer to singular or multiple spiny specimens will help.

Acknowledgments

The following horticulturists generously shared their time, cactus collections, gardens, advice, and expertise with me: Dan Johnson, Dave Ferguson, Donald Barnett Jr. and Sr., Gene Joseph, Jane Evans, Jon Weeks, Kelly Grummons, Lauren Springer Ogden, Mark Sitter, Miles Anderson, Panayoti Kelaidis, Scott Ogden, Sean Hogan, Steve Plath, and Tony Avent. I would like to particularly thank Matt Johnson, David Salman, and Greg Starr, who reviewed the manuscript and improved the finished product.

RIGHT: INDIAN FIG PLANTED UP AGAINST A COLORED WALL IN TUCSON'S BARRIO VIEJO NEIGHBORHOOD.

BELOW: KOENIG'S SNOWBALL COMING INTO BLOOM IN A HIGH-ELEVATION ROCK GARDEN.

ABOVE: THE COLORFUL AND LONG-PERSISTING YELLOW FRUIT OF THE FISHHOOK BARREL ARE COMPLEMENTED BY TRUE-BLUE WILDFLOWERS LIKE THESE DESERT BLUEBELLS.

RIGHT: WHITE SANDS CLARET CUP BLOOMING IN HABITAT AT WHITE SANDS NATIONAL MONUMENT IN NEW MEXICO.

Introduc

ABOVE:
A STOCKY LLOYD'S HEDGEHOG PUTS ON AN APRIL SHOW IN A DISPLAY GARDEN AT BACH'S CACTUS NURSERY IN TUCSON.

RIGHT:
LARGE PINK FLOWERS GRACE THE STEM TIPS OF THIS RAYONES HEDGEHOG IN AN ARIZONA COLLECTOR'S GARDEN.

tion

The cactus family is a group of plants containing around 2500 different species

—nearly a quarter of all succulent plant species. As the rubric goes: all cactus are succulents, but not all succulents are cactus. Cactus store water in fleshy stems, have waxy skin, and usually, though not always, have spines. Because cactus don't have traditional leaves, they photosynthesize with their stems. The stems can be shaped like columns, cylinders, paddles, rods, spheres, and barrels. Although the largest cactus species have trunks with diameters larger than telephone poles and reach heights of over 60 feet (18 m), the bulk of cactus species are low and mounding types that seldom grow taller than 18 inches (45 cm).

In place of leaves, most cactus have spines. The spines emerge from specialized parts of the skin called areoles. The spines themselves don't photosynthesize, but instead protect the plant from hungry herbivores and omnivores. Additionally, spines help direct water to the plant's root zone and provide shade and camouflage. The main spines tend to be stout, but some cactus species have secondary spines called glochids, which are small, hairlike, and irritating to remove from one's skin. Descriptions of main spines and glochids might lead you to think that cactus are fearsome plants, but a number of cactus are spineless (or nearly so) and welcome tactile contact. Even well-armed cactus species are not untouchable; more than a few cactus growers learn to handle them barehanded. For the rest of us, there are a host of specialized cactus tools that allow an amateur to grasp, lift, cut, and transplant even the most threatening cactus with ease.

A wholly New World family, all cactus species have genetic roots in the Americas. In North America, the epicenter of cactus diversity occurs in Mexico's Tehuacán Valley south of Mexico City. As one travels northward—eventually reaching the United States—the diversity of wild cactus decreases, with a few notable exceptions. The Sonoran Desert, the Mojave Desert, and the Chihuahuan Desert are all home to a broad and useful array of cactus species. Beyond the treasure trove of plants found in the southwestern states, a few species prefer the short-grass prairie and range as far north as Canada's Northwest Territories and east nearly to the shores of the Atlantic Ocean. With the exception of Maine, New Hampshire, and Vermont, cactus are native to all of the contiguous United States.

Observing cactus species in the wild tells us much about how they are best incorporated into gardens. Cactus grow in diverse habitats: you'll find them poking out of rocky outcrops, sprawling over sandy flats near oceans, mingling with grasses in prairie clay soil, and atop 11,000-foot (3300-m) mountains. If you choose the right species, it will be tolerant of harsh conditions. In the Southwest, when wild lands become severely degraded by overgrazing, cholla and prickly pears multiply and replace other plants that were eaten. They are survivor plants. When you look at cactus in the wild, it is helpful to notice what other plants are growing around them. While some grow alone in rubble or gravel, you are likely to find grasses, annual flowers, perennials, other succulents, and woody shrubs and trees growing next to cactus. Contrary to the way cactus are depicted in cartoons and advertising as widely spaced solo specimens, they are part of a plant community. By noting the companion plants that grow with cactus in the wild, you're more likely to have success when choosing companion plants in your garden.

CACTUS CONSERVATION

Throughout North American cactus have lost habitat as a result of human economic activities such as development, dams, agriculture, mining, and grazing. Some species have also been removed from habitat (legally and otherwise) to market to collectors and the nursery and landscape trade. If you are a gardener looking for cactus plants for your gardens, nine times out of ten the best conservation choice is to buy plants grown from seed at reputable cactus and succulent nurseries.

Seed-grown nursery plants are generally smaller and can be readily identified by their more or less "perfect" appearance. That is, nursery-grown cactus are generally free of the scars, broken spines, and tough corky tissue that are common on wild-collected cactus. Nursery-grown specimens are also not subjected to drought and extreme temperatures, so they tend to have a fresh, newly minted look. If you are unsure as to whether or not a plant is seed grown, ask. Buying seed-grown plants discourages smugglers from removing venerable wild plants from habitat. You vote with your dollars to take pressure off of wild populations.

There is one circumstance when buying wild-collected plants is a good conservation choice. Some cactus and succulent societies (those in Tucson and Las Vegas among them) have negotiated agreements with developers and mines that allow the salvaging of species that would otherwise be bladed under by heavy equipment. These wild-collected plants must have a state tag affixed to the plant for resale. Buying salvaged plants helps cactus and succulent societies finance robust conservation activities. Local cactus and succulent societies also promote reputable growers and are a great place to glean information about which species will thrive in your climate.

Planting and Care

▶ In terms of watering, pruning, and other sorts of plant maintenance, cactus are undoubtedly among the least-demanding group of plants on the planet. That said, like all plants, they require the least care when situated in an environment that mimics their natural habitat as much as possible. Once these conditions are provided, and the plants are established, cactus can be left on their own for weeks, or even months at a time with little or no care. Their reputation as tough plants is well deserved, but they are especially low maintenance if they are kept in robust health by paying attention to the following care tips.

Sun exposure

When we think of cactus, we probably imagine them stoically withstanding the full brunt of a relentless desert sun from dawn to dusk. And while it is true that most cactus appreciate full strong sunlight, in the Southwest and South, many cactus species enjoy some amount of shade on summer afternoons and when high temperatures exceed the century mark. In general, in the more northern parts of the country, cactus need all the sunlight you can provide, but in the hottest and driest climates, shading some species of cactus for a portion of the day is desirable.

Which species are likely to need some shade? Take a look at the plant: the more densely a species is covered with white reflective spines, the better equipped it is to withstand full sun. The more green flesh that is visible, the more likely it is to enjoy some amount of shade in hot sunny climates. If you see the flesh of your plant yellowing, this can be a sign of sun stress. Provide an adequate amount of shade and the yellow flesh will recover and re-green. If the flesh has gone from yellow to white, that flesh is dead and will not recover.

There are a few facts to remember. If you grow your plants under commercial shade cloth, you can produce a cactus with a normal appearance in up to 50 percent shade. Beyond 70 percent, the plant will lose its normal character. It may turn a darker color, or elongate to try to maximize its exposure to sunlight and ability to photosynthesize. Most commercial cactus nurseries grow cactus under some percentage of shade to speed their growth. These plants will need to be acclimated to full sun, which we will discuss.

If you grow potted cactus incompatible with your region's winters, you can move them indoors for the cold months. If you don't have a greenhouse or conservatory, a brightly sunlit room that stays above freezing will suit them well. Cactus aficionados in Colorado have been successful at wintering cactus in rooms whose winter temperatures hover between 40° and 50° F (4°–10° C). In a room this cool, little or no watering is needed until the plants are moved outdoors after the last frost. Although a south-facing windowsill has overwintered many a cactus collection, plants generally do better with more sun than can be provided indoors. The amount of light for cactus to truly thrive indoors year-around would seriously fade upholstery on furniture. Although cactus can be grown indoors, they often fail to thrive as indoor plants unless they are moved outdoors during the warm months when they are actively growing.

✳ CAM IDLING

▶ Cactus are hardwired with a water-efficient method of photosynthesis called CAM, which is an acronym for Crassulacean Acid Metabolism, but don't let that long name turn you off. CAM metabolism is just a fancy way of saying that the plant breathes at night rather than in the day. Over 90 percent of the world's plants photosynthesize and transpire (lose water through their leaves) during the day, so cactus and CAM plants are unusual in this regard. CAM plants keep their stomates (holes that exchange gas and water) closed in the day and open them during the nighttime when temperatures are lower and humidity is higher. Because of this adaptation cactus lose about one-tenth as much water as plants that photosynthesize in the standard way.

Transitioning shade-grown plants to full sun exposure

Most of the cactus specimens coming out of nurseries have been grown in partial shade. Plants from these conditions need to be sun-hardened. To get your cactus acclimated to full sun, mark the south side of the plant and plant it with the same orientation in your garden. For the first two to three weeks (especially in the summer) cover the southwest side of the plant with either 30 percent shade cloth or branches and sticks such as creosote bush branches. Gradually remove the shade cloth for a few hours per day until the plant has fully acclimated to the sun. If using branches, leave them in place until they decompose and fall away from the plant. If you are buying a plant that was grown in full sun, it is critically important that you plant it with the same orientation that it had in the nursery. Otherwise, it will be exceptionally prone to sunburn. This is especially true of plants such as saguaro cactus whose skin and spines become specially adapted on the sunny south and west sides of the plant to withstand intense light. To recap, plant orientation is more important for plants grown in full sun than it is for plants grown under some shade.

Cold hardiness

When it comes to cactus species, the one factor more than any other that will limit which of the plants in this book you can grow outdoors year-around is cold hardiness. Knowing what cold-hardiness zone you reside in will help you select plants. In cities like my hometown of Tucson, Arizona (zones 8b to 9a), our average annual minimum temperature is 20° to 30° F (7° to 1° C) and we experience an average of around twenty freezing nights each year. Seasonal timing and duration of cold are at least as important as the absolute low temperatures. This phenomenon has been well studied in the columnar saguaro cactus of Arizona: healthy saguaros have withstood 10° F (12°C) for a few hours, but after 12 hours of 20°F (7°C) temperatures, widespread damage and death were documented.

As you can see, the cold hardiness of cactus is a complex subject and one not easily treated with a broad brush. Suffice it to say that cactus collectors grow an enormous variety of species around the globe. From Tokyo and Bangkok, to Prague and Munich, to San Diego and Seattle—gardeners are growing cactus. Some climates will allow gardeners to plant more species in the ground than others, but cactus can be grown in containers everywhere.

Don't let the possibility of cold temperatures scare you away from cactus—even some of the less cold-hardy species. There are gardeners in Denver (zone 5) growing substantially sized saguaro cactus in pots (which are brought inside for winter) and some of the species listed here (not saguaros!) will happily take zone 3 (and even 2) cold even when unprotected and planted in the ground.

Frost protection

Strategies for cold protection vary by region. Because all cactus like winter sun, any frost protection devices should be removed between spells of cold weather so the plants will be in as much sun as can be provided.

BURLAP AND NURSERY POTS

In case of extreme cold, plants can be wrapped in burlap or frost cloth and covered with nursery pots to keep the burlap in place. Alternately, you can pack crumpled newsprint around your cactus for insulation and place a large nursery pot (such as a 15-gallon pot) over the top to keep the paper in place. Remember that even when taking pains to extensively insulate your cactus specimens, the added insulation can only provide approximately four to eight degrees F (two to four degrees C) of protection.

COVERED PORCHES AND OVERHANGS

In regions where cold nights arrive twenty or thirty times a year, move potted cactus underneath the solid cover of a porch for the coldest winter months. Ideally, the porch would be south-facing to allow the plants full solar gain in the winter. Placing cactus under the south-facing eaves of a house is also a great way to take advantage of the thermal gain from the house and avoid excess winter moisture around the plant.

FROST CLOTH

Commercially available frost cloths can add two to four degrees F (one to two degrees C) of protection for cactus either in the ground or in pots. To use, simply drape over plants.

SLOPE AND SOIL

Assuming that the species you have planted are adapted to the cold in your region, making sure your soil has sharp drainage is key to avoiding winter mortality.

STYROFOAM CUPS

In milder regions where columnar cactus are grown outdoors year-around, their growing tips can be protected with Styrofoam cups when temperatures fall into the twenties. Cups with a capacity of 32 or 64 ounces or larger can be used, depending on the girth of the cactus's cylindrical tips.

HOLIDAY-THEMED FROST PROTECTION FOR THESE COLUMNAR MEXICAN FENCEPOSTS INSULATES THEIR TENDER GROWING TIPS.

Cactus Planted in the Ground

▶ I keep a copy of a 1960s-era cartoon from *The New Yorker* on my office wall. In it, a homeowner is shown standing on a backyard patio. The backyard consists of a broad swath of manicured lawn surrounding a rugged, rocky, island-shaped planter filled with cactus. The cartoon depicts a crusty-looking prospector and laden donkey loping through the cactus island, and the homeowner chasing them out. I mention this cartoon because it illustrates a sort of old stereotype about what a cactus garden looks like—a segregated area consisting solely of cactus species and gravel—that is mostly outdated.

A new vibrant design model has emerged. Many of today's cactus gardens integrate cactus with drought-tolerant perennials, annuals, woody plants, and other succulents in a way that either imitates or abstracts natural patterns. This style—where cactus and succulents serve as living sculptures amongst a variety of other plants—is exceedingly handsome and has been employed at some of the country's most acclaimed private and botanic gardens. This is not to say that you can't have an interesting garden that is primarily dedicated to cactus. Certainly there are many cactus collectors who do just that, and do it with panache. But you can also grow cactus within a matrix of other plant types that form what we think of as a more traditional garden.

This contemporary method of integrating cactus into the broader garden takes a little planning and forethought. A key is making sure to group your cactus together with plants that have similar watering needs; whatever you plant that is adjacent to a cactus should be compatibly drought tolerant.

Knowing where you live is critically important to being successful growing cactus. As you might imagine, there are regions in which cactus are much easier to grow than others. For in-ground growing, cactus are best adapted to arid and semiarid areas that receive less than 30 inches of annual rainfall. In North America this includes the desert Southwest, the western Great Plains, the Intermountain West, Southern California, and Canada's Prairie Provinces. In these regions, you can even grow cactus in well-drained clay soils.

In parts of North America where more than 30 inches of rain falls annually, special measures have to be taken to successfully grow cactus in the ground. Remember, cactus roots dislike sitting in cold soggy soil. Most species will rot if subjected to these conditions. East of the 100th meridian, where a sizable portion of annual rainfall arrives in winter, try the following. Make a raised bed of pure, gritty soil or sharp sand up to 2 feet tall that will help water drain away from your cactus's roots. To further enhance the drainage, solar exposure, and warmth of your planting area, construct your fast-draining beds on

IN-GROUND GROWING IN THE CACTUS BELT

▶ For growing extensive cactus gardens in the ground, there is a magic belt that extends from Mexico, across the U.S. border to the deserts of the Southwest, and up into the Intermountain West. Throughout these areas, many cactus species thrive outdoors, unprotected, and planted more or less permanently in the ground. If you live in one of the cities listed here, count yourself lucky and take advantage of your situation by planting a proper cactus garden. If not, don't despair; there are many rewarding potted species as well as a handful of in-ground growers for areas across the majority of North America.

There are several U.S. cities where just about every species of cactus listed in this book can be planted successfully in the ground. This includes most of the columnar species that can't handle prolonged cold. These are largely cities that receive few, if any, hard frosts; they are all zone 9 or warmer. These warm cactus belt areas include Los Angeles, San Diego, Palm Springs, and Fresno, California; Yuma, Phoenix, and Tucson, Arizona; and central Las Vegas, Nevada (yes, the metropolitan core of Las Vegas is considerably warmer than outlying areas).

An intermediate cactus belt that is colder still allows gardeners a huge selection of plants for in-ground culture. This intermediate belt includes U.S. cities in zones 7 and 8 such as El Paso, Texas; Las Cruces and Albuquerque, New Mexico; Marfa and Odessa, Texas; and St. George, Utah.

The cold belt for in-ground cactus growing consists of cities in the Intermountain West. Although these cities are in zones 5 and 6, gardeners can still be very successful growing a great array of cactus species in the ground, although the plants need to be chosen and sited carefully. These cities include Boise, Idaho; Prescott, Arizona; Denver, Pueblo, and Grand Junction, Colorado; Reno, Nevada; Santa Fe, New Mexico; and Salt Lake City, Utah.

a south slope up against a home or building. If even those measures prove insufficient, potted plants can still be placed into the garden that will integrate with woody plants, grasses, and perennials. Growing cactus in containers gives you more cultural control and aesthetic options.

Watering cactus planted in the ground

The single most common cause of cactus mortality in landscapes is overwatering; often the gardener isn't aware that a cactus is being overwatered until it dies. This happened to a friend of mine when he planted a young saguaro cactus and surrounded it with perennial plants watered via a drip irrigation system three times per week. The saguaro itself was not irrigated. The cactus thrived for several years reaching a height of over 7 feet (2.1 m) tall, but one winter it fell in the middle of the night revealing a black rotten core from overwatering. On further examination, we determined that the saguaro's roots had reached into the perennials' irrigation.

Another potential killer of in-ground cactus plants is densely packed heavy soil that doesn't drain. The fact that cactus prefer well-drained soil is a universal principle that applies to all regions. To see if your soil drainage is adequate, dig a small 6-inch-deep hole near the spot you would like to plant. Fill the hole with water. It should drain within 30 minutes. If it does not, consider amending your soil with pumice, sharp sand, or some other gritty aggregate, and/or building mounds or a slope on which to plant your cactus.

Giving advice on a watering schedule is fraught with complications, due to regional differences in climate, soil, and exposure. In an attempt to demystify it as much as possible, here goes. Because cactus are warm-season growers, if they are watered it should only be during the frost-free portions of the year. In northerly cold-winter climates (including Salt Lake City, Denver, Santa Fe, Calgary, and Saskatoon), all cactus watering should cease by mid-August to avoid promoting new growth that would be prone to frost damage. In the warm pockets of the desert Southwest, cease watering in mid-October.

Another good tip to remember is that the larger and more mature the cactus, the less supplemental water it will need. In more northerly climes, including the Intermountain West, most gardeners growing cold-hardy cactus in-ground seldom, if ever, need to water their mature established plants. Exceptions to this rule would be seedlings and newly planted plants, which can be watered once a week for four to six weeks. Again, this advice is for northern climate gardeners.

If you live in the hot, arid Southwest, the following watering advice for established in-ground cactus applies: water your cactus twice a month during the frost-free portion of the year. Do not water in the rainy season. During the cool season (late autumn to early spring) watering just once or twice is adequate. Cactus have an extensive yet shallow root system; adjust the amount of water you apply accordingly.

Cactus in Containers

► In regions outside the prime in-ground cactus growing areas (the desert Southwest, the western Great Plains, the Intermountain West, and Southern California), cactus collections are most often potted. Potted cactus are typically planted singularly to highlight the attributes of one particular species although more than one species can be grouped together. An artfully potted collection displayed on a deck, patio, or bench is often the most interesting part of a garden. For a coherent look, avoid displaying your plants in black or green plastic nursery pots. Instead, purchase pots in a limited range of colors, but in different shapes and sizes.

One common myth about cactus culture in containers has been thoroughly debunked: the practice of putting a layer of gravel at the bottom of the pot. All that is needed is a pot with a drainage hole and either a single stone, or a screen (such as window screen) placed over the hole, to keep the soil mix from running out. Putting a layer of gravel at the bottom of the pot creates a "perched" water table that can rot cactus roots.

Cactus soil mixes for containers

When it comes to potting soil for cactus, good fast drainage is the number one concern. A watered cactus pot should drain in no longer than 30 seconds after watering. As a general rule, most cactus potting mixes have 25–50 percent organic matter with the balance made up of an inorganic, fast-draining material. The goal is to make a soil with a loose structure and good aeration, even when wet. When it comes to container soils for cactus, you have two options. Buy a bagged pre-blended soil mix labeled "cactus mix" from a garden center, or make your own. A high-quality bagged mix will be uniform and well drained. Bagged mixes are easy to buy and store in small quantities. Avoid cactus mixes with perlite—the little white beads in potting soil—that often rise to the surface of your soil making it unsightly. Instead look for mixes with pumice, which accomplishes the same drainage task without floating to the top.

You can make your own semi-custom potting mix by mixing 50 percent regular high quality potting soil with 45 percent pumice and 5 percent masonry sand. Some species of cactus—I'm thinking of a handful of mammillarias here—are so finicky about drainage that even cactus mix doesn't drain fast enough for them. For these consider Steve Plath's Ultra-Drain. Soil mixes are based at least as much on personal preferences and regional availability of soil components as they are on hard science. Since nearly every cactus grower has his or her soil recipe, I thought it would be best to give a sample of the sort of mixes professional cactus growers utilize.

MILES ANDERSON Anderson's Miles' To Go specializes in cactus for mail order. This mix is for a 5-gallon-bucket-sized amount of soil: Fill bucket 3/4 full with 3/8-inch-minus pumice, and the remaining 1/4 bucket with pine bark mulch. Amend mixture with 2/3 cup pelletized dolomitic limestone, 1/3 cup pelletized gypsum, 1/3 cup potassium sulfate, and 1/4 cup slow-release fertilizer. Miles grows a wide range of species in this mix.

KELLY GRUMMONS For this mix, start with 3 cubic feet of good quality potting mix (Kelly uses Metro Mix 380) and 3 cubic feet 1/4-inch scoria. Add 1 cup Planters II micronutrients. Kelly is the proprietor of Timberline Gardens in the Denver metro area. He cultivates larges quantities of prickly, cholla, and beehive cactus in his soil mix.

GENE JOSEPH AND JANE EVANS This team's mix is 50 percent pumice, 20 percent peat moss, 20 percent mulch (decomposed fir bark), 5 percent sand, and 5 percent vermiculite. Growing everything from living stones to aloes to torch cactus, Gene and Jane have developed this proven and versatile mix at their Plants for the Southwest nursery. They also sell their mix in bags at the nursery.

DAVID SALMAN The founder of Santa Fe Greenhouses and High Country Gardens catalog, David blends 5 parts bark-based soilless mix, 2 parts scoria, and 2 parts course sand (not plaster sand). His long love of cactus and experience in greenhouses, gardens, and the mail-order business have contributed to the development of his cactus mix.

STEVE PLATH The owner of Signature Botanica nursery outside Phoenix, Steve developed his Ultra-Drain mix after discovering that growing certain species of Mammillaria in straight calcined clay worked wonders where a normal cactus mix failed. "I could water them every day and not rot them," Steve said. Calcined clay is a clay that is fired to 1200°–1400° F (650°–760° C). It looks like light tan gravel but is extremely absorbent. Most people are familiar with calcined clay because it is the main (and often only) ingredient in kitty litter and bagged oil-spill absorbents.

MARK SITTER Mark is the owner of B & B Cactus in Tucson. He uses a simple mix of 50 percent horticultural-grade pumice and 50 percent forest mulch. Both the pumice and forest mulch are un-screened and contain coarse to fine-sized particles.

GREG STARR Greg's mix is 60 percent pumice, 20 percent sharp sand, and 20 percent 1/4-inch minus compost. Starr is a noted horticulturist and succulent expert and the owner of Starr Nursery in Tucson. His soil mix has proven successful for growing numerous agave and cactus species.

Top Dressing

Spreading mulch, or top-dressing, on the surface of the soil in your containers gives them a tidy appearance and helps reduce water loss through evaporation. For large specimen plants in large pots, coarse gravel from 3/4 to 1 inch in diameter can be spread up to 2 inches thick. For smaller plants, 1/4-inch gravel, or finer, looks best. To ensure the best results, choose screened gravel and rinse off the dust before applying it as a top dressing.

Container selection

Choosing the right pot for your climate, particularly the rainfall patterns of your climate, is important. When selecting a pot for cactus culture, the goal is to choose a vessel that will allow water to move quickly through the root zone and exit the pot, at the same time maintaining somewhat even soil moisture from the top to bottom of the container. Your pot should facilitate an "open" soil with plenty of oxygen for your cactus's root zones and a gritty substantial mix that gives your spiny plants' roots something to firmly grip.

SHAPE AND SIZE To understand the differences in the way water moves in a tall, narrow pot versus a low, shallow pot, picture a wet rectangular sponge. If the sponge is held vertically, more of the water will migrate to the bottom of the sponge leaving a drier area near the top. When the sponge is laid flat, the moisture levels from top to bottom are more consistent. This extra water that hangs out at the bottom of pots is often referred to as a "perched water table" and is considered something to be avoided. Saucers exacerbate perched water tables and should be avoided for cactus culture. Because of perched water tables, most cactus growers tend to favor low, shallow pots.

TO BREATHE OR NOT TO BREATHE? Although you might think that cactus would always prefer pots that are porous (breathable), it really depends on the region where you garden. As a general rule, in areas that receive more than 20 inches of annual rainfall, permeable pots work best. In more arid regions, impermeable pots tend to perform better.

IMPERMEABLE POTS Examples of impermeable pots include high-fired (typically fired between 2100° and 2500° F, 1150° and 1370° C) ceramic pots—often called stoneware pots, which are usually glazed. If you flick these pots with a finger they make a bell-like, pinging sound, which you wouldn't hear from a low-fired pot. Although they cost more than low-fired pots, high-fired pots are known for their durability and usually resist cracking in freezing weather better than their terra cotta counterparts. Plastic pots are also impermeable, although finding attractive plastic pots is not easy. Other impermeable pot materials include fiberglass, resin, metal, and cast concrete.

POROUS POTS The porous pots you are likely most familiar with, and probably already own a few of, are Italian terra cotta. These pots wick moisture through their sides and dry out more quickly than impermeable pots. Another type of permeable pot would be low-fired Mexican clay pots. These typically have thicker walls than terra cotta pots and are often coated with black asphalt emulsion on the inside to make them impermeable. Lastly, hypertufa, a stone-like pot made with various quantities of dry cement, peat moss, vermiculite, and water, is a porous material often used in wetter portions of the country to house cactus and succulent plants.

Transplanting potted cactus

Up-potting or shifting is moving a cactus from a smaller pot to a larger one. This is best done after the last frost in spring or in early summer in cooler northern climates; or in spring, summer, or early autumn in the hot regions of the Southwest. The logic behind these suggested transplanting times is to up-pot the plant at a time of year when it has time to actively grow and re-root before cold weather hits. When choosing the new pot, it is best to choose a pot just slightly larger than the old pot. Remember, cactus don't mind having their roots restricted (or under-potted). Putting a small cactus in an oversized pot may lead to root rot. When up-potting, always remove the existing soil around the roots and trim the roots as well. This bare-root planting method ensures that the cactus's roots are re-invigorated and grow directly into the fresh potting mix—it is also recommended when planting nursery-grown cactus in the ground. After transplanting, wait a few days to water so that any damaged roots can heal over.

Showing Cactus

► Carefully arranging your prized cactus specimens in pots—or staging—is fun and rewarding. It is similar to bonsai and flower arranging in that the finished product is considered art and is designed to wow. The practice began at cactus and succulent shows sponsored by cactus clubs and the Cactus and Succulent Society of America (CSSA), to show off particularly well-grown and exceptional cactus specimens. Serious cactus collectors compete for ribbons on a 100-point scale. Plants are judged for their quality and health (60 percent), arrangement in the pot (20 percent), plant size and age (15 percent), and correct nomenclature (5 percent). The overall goal is to combine cactus, rocks, gravel, and pottery in a way that resembles a living sculpture and perhaps mimics how the plant would grow in its native habitat. As the cactus plants grow, up-pot them every 3 to 5 years giving them fresh soil with each re-potting.

HERE ARE SOME TIPS FOR STAGING CACTUS

- -

▶ **Choose just one species of cactus per container.** Your goal is to highlight the best attributes of one plant rather than to show off a bunch of different species in one pot. The latter is dish gardening, which is another judged category.

▶ **Remember that the cactus plant itself is the most important element in the composition.** Select robust specimens and choose plants with the most interesting characteristics and the least flaws.

▶ **Choose a pot whose shape and color complement the plant.** In the past, judges have considered bright colors that distract from the plant bad form. Today, bright colors are more accepted provided they complement the cactus plants. That said, the predominant pot colors you'll see at shows will be earth tones.

▶ **Especially with handmade pots, find the front of the pot.**

▶ **Each cactus tends to have a front as well**—one side that will be the most attractive. Plant the cactus so its front aligns with the front of the pot, toward the viewer. Additionally, some species may look best when planted leaning toward the viewer.

▶ **If you are shooting for a naturalistic look, consider placing the plant off-center.**

▶ **Plant high in the pot and use rocks to brace the plant in place.**

▶ **If your pot is too large, place large rocks around its circumference.**

▶ **Have a variety of top-dressing sizes on hand.** For large containers, you may want to use a large (1- or 3/8-inch diameter) gravel, while for smaller pots, a fine anthill-sized gravel might look best. Always rinse gravel before application.

▶ **Use a fine jet of water to spray off dust and soil particles.**

▶ **Remove any weeds, broken spines, leaf debris, and spider webs.** In judged CSSA competitions, sometimes the difference between winning and losing can be a single broken spine!

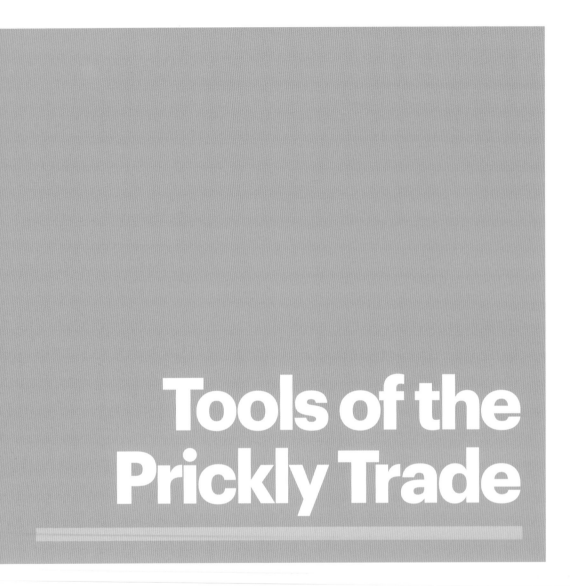

Tools of the Prickly Trade

► A few hard-boiled cactophiles work with cactus barehanded, but for most gardeners, some sort of protection and tools are a necessity and make the experience pleasurable. With just a few tools, you will be able to handle cactus chores such as potting, pruning, harvesting, weeding, and transplanting with ease. Several cactus tools are also used for surgery, but don't let that worry you. Some of my favorites:

CACTUS SAW A cactus saw is a long handled saw with an angled blade. It is great for pruning off hard-to-reach prickly pear pads or taking off old agave leaves.

COOKING TONGS Inexpensive cooking tools are available at nearly any supermarket and are great for harvesting prickly pear cactus fruit and pads. They can also be used to handle and transplant small ball-shaped cactus.

GLOVES I prefer heavy-duty welder's gloves. These affordable thick leather gloves extend halfway up your forearm and can be used to pick up a barrel cactus or any smaller cactus as needed. I've seen cactus nursery workers wrap duct tape around the fingers of regular gardening gloves to handle cactus and this is another cheap and easy method. Keep in mind that while these gloves will protect you from the big spines, the small hairlike glochids can work their way into many gloves. When handling cactus with lots of glochids, you may want to consider one of the other tools listed here. For handling smaller cactus without glochids, regular gardening gloves are lighter and give you better tactile sense.

HEMOSTAT Like a long pair of locking tweezers. Great for grabbing the lip of cactus pots when they are imbedded in flats with other cactus. Also can be used for weeding.

KITCHEN SIEVE OR COLANDER Use to rinse the dust and fine particles off of gravel top dressing.

LAZY SUSAN If you get serious about staging show cactus specimens, a lazy Susan makes a nice platform on which to artfully work with cactus in containers. It allows you to easily view the plant from all angles.

LONG TWEEZERS (FORCEPS) For removing leaves, flowers, and debris from cactus thorns, long tweezers are indispensable. They are also are the quickest and most accurate tool to use for weeding. They are typically available in lengths of 6, 8, 10, 12, 15, and 18 inches. I find that the 6- or 8-inch sizes are adequate for working with most cactus species.

OLD CARPET A section of old carpet can be used like a stretcher to move either columnar or barrel-shaped cactus.

OLD GARDEN HOSE A 3- to 6-foot length of old garden hose is excellent for moving and transplanting columnar cactus such as small saguaros. To use as a sling, one person lassos the top portion of the plant with the hose, the other handles the roots.

SMALL HAND SCOOP For use with potting soil mixes and for putting gravel top-dressing in pots.

WATER BREAKER A watering device such as a wand with a water-breaker head that evenly and gently distributes water will allow you to water your potted cactus without blasting the gravel top dressing onto the patio.

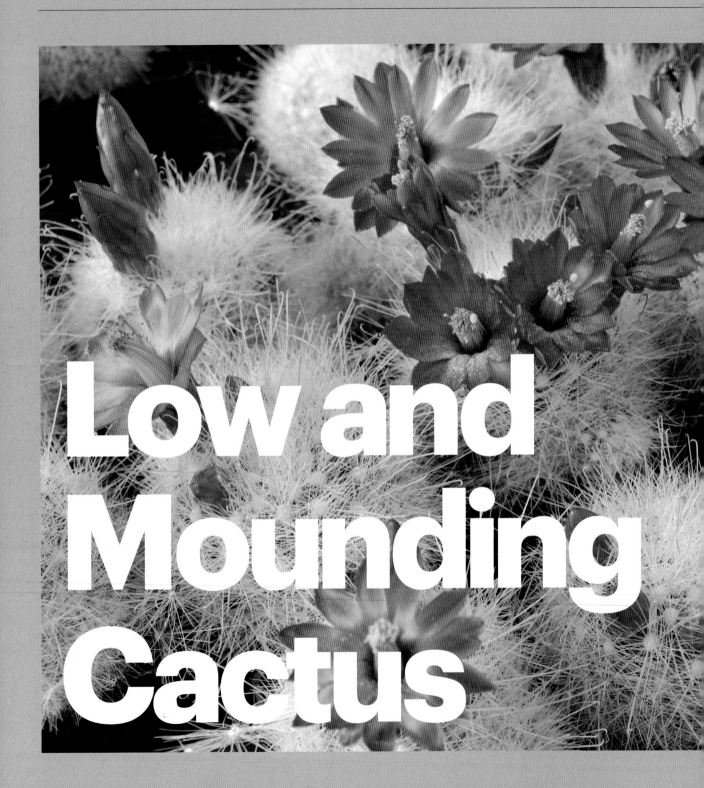

Low and Mounding Cactus

MORPHOLOGY—THE SHAPE OF THINGS—is how this book approaches the cactus world, and that is how I've organized the one hundred species featured. Since cactus are typically incorporated into gardens as living sculptures, I thought that it would be best to group the plants into sections by size and form, rather than a simple A to Z list by botanical name. We begin with low and mounding species.

The low and mounding group is graced with a dazzling scope of forms, varieties, and colors. Additionally, many in this group are among the most cold hardy of all the species covered in this book. The plants in this section have evocative common names: beehive, hedgehog, and pincushion cactus, but also include lesser-known garden treasures such as plants in the genus *Thelocactus*. Rock gardeners prize many of the species covered in this section and work them into rockeries and containers. Low and mounding types are small, with most growing less than 18 inches (45 cm) tall; because of their petite size, they are excellent for potted collections and for wedging between other arid-adapted plants. Low and mounding cactus are among the most versatile of all cactus and are increasingly seen incorporated into dry-garden plantings mixed with perennials, bulbs, ornamental grasses, and woody shrubs.

TEXAS RAINBOW CACTUS BLOOMING ALONG WITH POPPIES AT THE DENVER BOTANIC GARDENS.

Widely admired by cactus lovers for their substantial flowers and clustering stems (on most species), the genus contains between 44 and 60-some species—depending on whether botanists lump or split *Echinocereus*. The native range of hedgehogs extends south to north from south-central Mexico to Kansas, South Dakota, and Wyoming; east to west they range from Kansas to eastern California.

In gardens the hedgehogs are excellent potted or worked into rock gardens. Their flowers range from chartreuse to carmine red and when multiple species are included in a garden, one can easily have hedgehogs in bloom for consecutive months. In size, they range from miniature plants only a few inches high and wide to burly species a couple of feet high and several feet across. An aspect of hedgehog cactus rarely discussed in horticultural literature is the excellent taste of their fruit—sweet with crunchy seeds, sometimes compared in flavor to strawberries.

ENGELMANN'S HEDGEHOG BLOOMS NEXT TO A DRY-STACKED ROCK WALL AT THE DESERT BOTANICAL GARDEN, PHOENIX, ARIZONA.

ENGELMANN'S HEDGEHOG SIDLES UP TO BRITTLEBUSH IN ANZA-BORREGO NATIONAL PARK.

Hedgehog Heaven

Echinocereus bonkerae

bonker hedgehog

Perhaps the deepest purple flowers of all the hedgehogs (although some individuals bloom magenta or pink) combined with an attractive net of short white spines make this a highly desirable garden species.

NATIVE HABITAT	MATURE SIZE	HARDINESS	FLOWERING SEASON
Restricted to central and southeastern Arizona	8 inches (20 cm) high and 12–24 inches (30–60 cm) wide.	Zone 7	Mid- to late spring

BONKER HEDGE-HOG COMING INTO BLOOM IN A FRONT-YARD ROCK GARDEN.

► Bonker hedgehog is easy to distinguish from other hedgehog species, with its shorter white spines. The compact, neatly organized spines give the plant a tidier, less-shaggy appearance than other species. It grows in open grasslands and occasionally beneath trees and shrubs. The silky, dark purple flowers stand out particularly well against the bonker hedgehog's white spines and dark green body. Bonker hedgehog was formerly lumped in with *Echinocereus fendleri* and *E. fasciculatus* but now stands alone as its own species. It is almost always sold in the trade as *E. bonkerae*.

CULINARY VALUE
Fruit with tasty edible flesh

DESIGN SUGGESTIONS
The body of this plant is handsome enough to showcase in an urn next to a walkway. Better yet, flank a walkway with a pair of bonker hedgehogs either in pots or in the ground. It looks good planted adjacent to native grasses with airy seed heads such as purple three awn (*Aristida purpurea*) and alkali sacaton (*Sporobolus airoides*).

CULTIVATION
Full bright sun makes for the best landscape specimens. Plants grown in less light tend to take on an undesirable lumpy form.

Echinocereus carmenensis

chocolate-scented hedgehog

A small single-stemmed (solitary) hedgehog with intensely fragrant yellow-green (and sometimes red-brown) flowers that smell of sweet chocolate.

NATIVE HABITAT	MATURE SIZE	HARDINESS	FLOWERING SEASON
Sierra Del Carmen, Coahuila, Mexico	6 inches (15 cm) tall with stems 2.5 inches (6.4 cm) in diameter	 Zone 8	Mid- to late spring

➤ A formerly rare plant, chocolate-scented hedgehog is now readily available at several cactus nurseries. The plants are seed grown with seed collected by Stephen Brack in the Sierra Del Carmen Mountains (4900–5600 feet, 1470–1680 m) in northern Mexico. Chocolate-scented hedgehog is usually solitary with spines that radiate out from the body in a circular fashion.

DESIGN SUGGESTIONS

Place this plant in a location close to entryways and walkways where the curious scent of the flowers will pique the attention of passersby.

For a double-dose of chocolate scent, plant the perennial chocolate flower (*Berlandiera lyrata*) in proximity to chocolate-scented hedgehog.

CULTIVATION

Provide quick-draining gritty soil and withhold water during the cold winter months.

CHOCOLATE-SCENTED HEDGEHOG NEARING PEAK BLOOM AT MILES' TO GO NURSERY IN TUCSON.

Showy horizontal bands of spines that alternate between white and red, plus big-ass yellow flowers make it a garden gem.

Echinocereus dasyacanthus

Texas rainbow cactus

NATIVE HABITAT	**MATURE SIZE**	**HARDINESS**	**FLOWERING SEASON**
Texas, New Mexico	Stems 5–10 inches (13–25 cm), occasionally up to 18 inches (45 cm) high and 24 inches (60 cm) across	Zone 6b	Mid- to late spring

► The Texas rainbow cactus has exceptional cold hardiness and outsized yellow or orange (rarely pink), wine-cup-shaped flowers. It is an awesome and underused species. With its showy horizontal banding, the body is handsome when out of flower; in flower, it stops traffic. Each flower remains open for several days, closing partially at night. Texas rainbow is often solitary, but it sometimes clusters, forming a plant with 3–10 stems.

DESIGN SUGGESTIONS

If you live in a dry region, try planting it in the ground. It is striking when planted en masse with other hedgehog species, particularly the red-flowering claret cup hedgehog, which blooms at around the same time. David Salman of High Country Gardens plants his Texas rainbow hedgehog next to a low ground cover, *Aethionema caespitosa* or *Veronica bombycina*.

CULTIVATION

Tucson horticulturist Matt Johnson recommends planting at the base of creosote bushes and avoiding excessive overhead water, particularly during the hot, humid summer months.

NOTABLE VARIETIES, FORMS, AND SUBSPECIES:

For greatest cold hardiness, look for plants grown from seed collected in San Miguel County, New Mexico. This disjunct population is more than 200 miles north of the next closest location of Texas rainbow cactus.

A YOUNG TEXAS RAINBOW CACTUS BLOOMS NEXT TO THE PERENNIAL *AETHIONEMA CAESPITOSA* IN DAVID SALMAN'S SANTA FE GARDEN.

Echinocereus engelmannii

Engelmann's hedgehog

A wonderfully shaggy creature with spines that come in red, yellow, mahogany, black, and white.

NATIVE HABITAT

Widespread in the southwest U.S. and northwestern Mexico, it grows in the Sonoran, Mojave, and even in parts of the southern Great Basin deserts.

MATURE SIZE

12 inches (30 cm) high, forming clusters 3 feet (0.9 m) or more across

HARDINESS

Zone 7

FLOWERING SEASON

Late winter to late spring

► This robust hedgehog is remarkable for its colorful hairy spines that make it attractive in the garden regardless of the season. Due to its large range, Englemann's hedgehog varies in spine length, color, and spine density. As a garden cactus it is hard to beat; one of the earliest blooming species, it will produce flowers over a four-week period sometime between February and May. The large 2- to 3-inch-wide flowers are most often a rich magenta but are occasionally lavender colored. A long bloomer, Engelmann's hedgehog produces flowers that remain open for over a week. The excellent fruit is reported to have been eaten by the Hohokam tribe, and more recent native tribes in Central Arizona. I can attest to its excellent flavor.

ENGELMANN'S HEDGEHOG BLOOMS NEXT TO A DRY-STACKED ROCK WALL AT THE DESERT BOTANICAL GARDEN, PHOENIX, ARIZONA.

CULINARY VALUE

An exotic culinary treat, the juicy fig-sized fruit tastes of strawberry and vanilla. When ripe, the spines fall off the scarlet fruit easily and can be flicked off with a stick or a brave and careful finger.

DESIGN SUGGESTIONS

Superb in rock gardens or in broad shallow pots

CULTIVATION

One of the very easiest hedgehogs to grow; in low-light climates it may be stubborn to come to flower, which is okay since the spines are an attraction on their own.

NOTABLE VARIETIES, FORMS, AND SUBSPECIES

For a zone 5, cold-hardy form, seek out *Echinocereus engelmannii* subsp. *variegatus*, a much smaller clumper from northern Arizona.

Echinocereus fendleri

Fendler hedgehog

Exceptionally large, dark pink flowers and extreme cold hardiness make Fendler hedgehog one of the best garden species.

NATIVE HABITAT

New Mexico, southeastern Arizona, southeastern Colorado; Sonora and Chihuahua, Mexico

MATURE SIZE

5–8 inches (13–20 cm) high and 6–20 inches (15–51 cm) across

HARDINESS

Zone 5

FLOWERING SEASON

Mid- to late spring

► Fendler hedgehog is one of the smaller members of the hedgehog genus, but the outsized flowers make up for the modest stature of the plant's body. Each magenta-colored flower is nearly 3 inches wide and stays open for over one week. The spines are mostly white or gray, save the central spines, which have dark tips. In some populations the plants have very ornamental, pure black and white spines.

CULINARY VALUE

The fruit, similar to the fruit of *Echinocereus engelmannii*, are juicy and taste of strawberries when ripe. Also like *E. engelmannii*, the spines easily fall off the fruit when it is ripe.

DESIGN SUGGESTIONS

Awesome in hypertufa trough gardens as a single specimen, or in a garden surrounded by perennials from the short grass prairie, such as sundrops (*Calylophus hartwegii*), Angelita daisy (*Tetraneuris acaulis*), and dotted blazing star (*Liatris punctata*).

CULTIVATION

Slow-growing and small, taking 4–5 years to flower if grown from seed

NOTABLE VARIETIES, FORMS, AND SUBSPECIES

Plants grown from seed originating in eastern New Mexico and southeastern Colorado are the most cold hardy.

A TROUGH-LOAD OF BLOOMING FENDLER HEDGEHOG, SURROUNDED BY A YELLOW-BLOOMING CORE-OPSIS SPECIES AT DENVER BOTANIC GARDENS.

Echinocereus knippelianus

peyote verde

Virtually spineless, nearly flat as a pancake, and graced with an eerie black-green color, this cactus is a highly desirable curiosity. Its unfortunate species name is guaranteed to make schoolboys of the Bart Simpson ilk snicker.

NATIVE HABITAT	**MATURE SIZE**	**HARDINESS**	**FLOWERING SEASON**
Coahuila and Nuevo León, Mexico, above 7200 feet (2160 m)	2–4 inches (5.1–10 cm) high and 4–10 inches (10–25 cm) wide	Zone 6	Spring

A SIZABLE COLONY OF PEYOTE VERDE IN A ROCK GARDEN SETTING AT DENVER BOTANIC GARDENS.

► Peyote verde grows from a huge underground taproot, but the plant barely rises above the ground. In the wild, it is typically a single-headed plant, but in cultivation it may develop many heads. The plant has a few flimsy spines that usually drop off as the plant matures, so for all intents and purposes it is non-pokey. In shape, it looks similar to regular peyote (*Lophophora williamsii*) and is evidently used as a less-powerful hallucinogen by indigenous people. Its flowers are fairly large and pale pink but not nearly as interesting as the color and form of the body of the plant.

CULINARY VALUE

Hallucinogenic, but reportedly with milder effects than regular peyote

DESIGN SUGGESTIONS

This plant looks great planted as a trio in a low bowl set on a bench, where its curious form and color can be appreciated up close. Experiment with gravel colors in a pot to highlight its green-black body.

CULTIVATION

Peyote verde grows from a fleshy tuberous taproot. Like regular peyote, it can be propagated from cuttings.

NOTABLE VARIETIES, FORMS, AND SUBSPECIES

Echinocereus knippelianus var. *reyesii* has larger and deeper colored flowers; *E. knippelianus* var. *kruegeri* is a form notable for its clumping, smaller stature, and flesh-colored flowers.

Echinocereus longisetus subsp. *delaetii*
(Also sold as *Echinocereus delaetii* var. *delaetii*)

viejitos

Wavy, white, hairlike stems and outsized pink flowers distinguish viejitos from its relatives in the genus.

NATIVE HABITAT

Limestone slopes of Coahuila, Mexico in the Sierra Madre Oriental above 5900 feet (1700 m)

MATURE SIZE

12–14 inches (30–35 cm) tall and up to 3 feet (0.9 m) across

HARDINESS

Zone 8

FLOWERING SEASON

Late spring through early summer

► Its Spanish common name, viejitos, or little old man, is a fairly apt description of this unusual hedgehog—the only plant in the genus with long curling hairs. Over time, it can form yard-wide clumps comprised of as many as 50 stems, but in cultivation it is typically smaller. Nearly 3-inch-wide, slightly drooping pink flowers with yellow centers stand out against the kinky long spines; in cultivation, some collectors report that it is difficult to coax into flower, but in Arizona it flowers easily when grown in the ground or pots.

DESIGN SUGGESTIONS

Plant alongside tough perennial wildflowers such as bahia (*Bahia abinthifolia*) and Black-foot daisy (*Melampodium leucanthum*) as pictured in the photo.

CULTIVATION SUGGESTIONS:

Needs quick-draining soil and full sun for best flowering

VIEJITOS BLOOMING AMONG BAHIA AND BLACK-FOOT DAISY AT TUCSON BOTANICAL GARDENS.

With its golden spines and bright green body, the golden hedgehog is considered by many to be the most dazzling of all the *Echinocereus* species.

Echinocereus nicholii subsp. *nicholii*
(Also sold as *Echinocereus engelmannii* var. *nicholii*)

golden hedgehog

NATIVE HABITAT

Mountains in central Arizona and northwestern Sonora, Mexico. Common in the Silver Bell Mountains near Tucson and in Organ Pipe National Monument.

MATURE SIZE

12–24 inches (30–60 cm) high and 2–4 feet (0.6–1.2 m) wide

HARDINESS

Zone 8

FLOWERING SEASON

Mid- to late spring

▶ The golden hedgehog is a big, robust plant with stems that typically curve upright and can reach 2 feet tall. The bright green body of the plant is partially obscured with dense golden spines and creates an almost chartreuse appearance—the hedgehog color equivalent of the golden barrel cactus. The flowers, while small, are pink or pale lavender, and contrast splendidly with the yellow spines.

CULINARY VALUE

Like many of the hedgehogs, the ripe fruit makes excellent eating.

DESIGN SUGGESTIONS

If possible, place the golden hedgehog where early morning or late evening light will illuminate the spines from behind.

CULTIVATION

When grown in temperate regions, the golden hedgehog is reported to be more free-flowering than *Echinocereus engelmannii*. For best flowering and spine coloration, grow in full strong sunlight. The golden hedgehog will also thrive in reflected heat.

NOTABLE VARIETIES, FORMS, AND SUBSPECIES

Subspecies *llanuraensis*, found only near Guaymas, Sonora, Mexico, has crimson flowers.

THE GOLDEN HEDGEHOG WITH SPINES AGLOW, GROWING IN HABITAT
IN THE SILVER BELL MOUNTAINS NEAR TUCSON, ARIZONA.

LADYFINGER CACTUS BLOOMING FULL-STOP IN HABITAT ON A GRASSY MESQUITE FLAT IN THE CHIHUAHUAN DESERT.

One of the few cactus that prefers to grow in shady undergrowth, and forms a large, ground-cover-style mat of stems.

Echinocereus pentalophus

ladyfinger cactus; alicoche

NATIVE HABITAT	MATURE SIZE	HARDINESS	FLOWERING SEASON
South Texas through northern Mexico, as far south as Querétaro	12 inches (30 cm) high, spreading to 3–4 feet (0.9–1.2 m) across	Zone 8	Mid- to late spring

► This unusual prostrate hedgehog has medium-green arms that sprawl out on the ground. The flowers are tri-colored with pink tepals, white throats, and dark-green stamens. Each flower opens at noon and blooms for a couple of days, closing each night. Because of its preference for shade, ladyfinger cactus can be grown in lower light conditions than most other cactus species.

DESIGN SUGGESTIONS
Excellent under the canopy of mesquite and oak trees. Also good in tall pots where its stems can trail down. Additionally, ladyfinger cactus are one of the best choices for hanging baskets.

CULTIVATION
Best in partial shade or at least filtered light

NOTABLE VARIETIES, FORMS, AND SUBSPECIES
Subspecies *leonensis* has erect rather than prostrate stems.

Grow it for its 2-inch-long glassy white spines, hot pink flowers that bloom reliably each year, and miniature size.

Echinocereus rayonensis

Rayones hedgehog

NATIVE HABITAT	MATURE SIZE	HARDINESS	FLOWERING SEASON
Rayones Valley, Nuevo León, Mexico	5–7 inches (13–18 cm) high and 1 foot (30 cm) wide	Zone 8	Early to midsummer

► Rayones hedgehog is such a white, hairy cactus that its stems are obscured by its dense spination. Its spines are fine, stiff, and glassine white. Its thin arms grow relatively upright. Its small size (it is often described as dwarf) and unusual color have made it an instant hit with collectors. It blooms hot pink to magenta flowers reliably in cultivation, and begins blooming at a young age.

DESIGN SUGGESTIONS

Excellent in a low bowl or if planted in the ground, grown adjacent to the narrow leaves and light blue flowers of *Penstemon amphorellae*.

CULTIVATION

Rayones hedgehog is a reliable bloomer in cultivation.

LARGE PINK FLOWERS GRACE THE STEM TIPS OF THIS RAYONES HEDGEHOG IN AN ARIZONA COLLECTOR'S GARDEN.

Echinocereus reichenbachii var. *albispinus*
(Also sold as *Echinocereus reichenbachii baileyi* var. *albispinus*)

white lace cactus; Oklahama lace cactus

This tiny clumping cactus is Santa Fe nurseryman David Salman's favorite. It has pure-white spines and sweet-smelling pale pink flowers, is easy to grow, and is among the very most cold-hardy and moisture-tolerant cactus.

NATIVE HABITAT	MATURE SIZE	HARDINESS	FLOWERING SEASON
Johnston County, Oklahoma	2–4 inches (5.1–10 cm) tall, clumping to 6–10 inches (15–25 cm) across	Zone 5	Early to midsummer

► A superb low-mounding plant for cold-winter areas. In habitat, white lace cactus grows in the rock outcroppings and among grasses in the short-grass prairie. White lace cactus has spines that do not lie as close to the stem as other varieties of lace cactus giving it a bristly appearance. Its spines are also notably brighter and more numerous. Individual stems have a diameter from 1.5 to 3.5 inches (3.8–9 cm). The fragrant pink chintz-colored flowers bloom close to the end of its stems.

DESIGN SUGGESTIONS

A broad, low, glazed bowl with three or more plants clustered together makes an exceptional focal point. Also nice interplanted in the garden with smaller short-grass prairie perennials like *Scutellaria resinosa*, *Hymenoxys scaposa*, and *Oenothera* species.

CULTIVATION

Although the white lace cactus is easy to grow, it enjoys a rest period in winter (abstain from winter watering, as you would do with most cactus species).

NOTABLE VARIETIES, FORMS, AND SUBSPECIES

Another very similar form of *Echinocereus reichenbachii* var. *albispinus* is found in Troy and Johnston County, Oklahoma.

WHITE LACE CACTUS THRIVING IN A BLUE GLAZED POT IN DAVID SALMAN'S SANTA FE, NEW MEXICO, GARDEN. THIS PARTICULAR PLANT WAS GROWN FROM SEED COLLECTED IN TISHOMINGO, OKLAHOMA.

Echinocereus rigidissimus
(Also sold as *Echinocereus pectinatus* var. *rubispinus*)

Arizona rainbow hedgehog; Sonoran rainbow cactus

NATIVE HABITAT

Arizona, the southwest corner of New Mexico, and northern Mexico

MATURE SIZE

3–12 inches (7.6–30 cm) high and 2–5 (5.1–13 cm) inches wide

HARDINESS

Zone 8a

FLOWERING SEASON

Late spring to early summer

► Usually a solitary non-clumping grower, the Arizona rainbow cactus is at home in grass-land and oak woodland. It looks smart growing among native grasses. The short, dense spines fan out flat against the body of the plant, making it a cactus that you can handle without gloves. The flowers are an intense dark pink with a white throat.

DESIGN SUGGESTIONS

Excellent grouped together in a pot or planted naturalistically with little blue stem and grama grasses, as well as *Agave palmeri*

CULTIVATION

Requires an exceedingly well-drained soil, intense sunlight, and hot summer temperatures to be its best

NOTABLE VARIETIES, FORMS, AND SUBSPECIES

Echinocereus pectinatus var. *rubispinus*, desirable for its very large flowers and darker, ruby-colored banding, is a Mexican variety which is more common at nurseries than the straight species.

ARIZONA RAINBOW HEDGEHOG GROWING IN-SITU IN A SHORT-GRASS PRAIRIE OF MIXED GRAMA GRASSES IN SOUTHEASTERN ARIZONA.

One of the few hedgehogs with strongly orange-colored flowers, Lloyd's hedgehog is a garden showstopper.

Echinocereus ×roetteri var. *neomexicanus*
(Also sold as *Echinocereus lloydii*)

Lloyd's hedgehog

NATIVE HABITAT	**MATURE SIZE**	**HARDINESS**	**FLOWERING SEASON**
Common between Ft. Stockton, Texas, and Big Bend National Park; also in New Mexico's Jarilla Mountains	8 to 14 inches (20 to 35 cm) high and as wide as 1 to 2 feet (30 to 60cm) across	Zone 6b	Mid- to late spring

▶ Lloyd's hedgehog has a stocky body with several arms. It is a naturally occurring hybrid between the claret cup and the Texas rainbow cactus. A relatively rare plant, it comes from places where the ranges of two hedgehog species collide creating hybrid swarms of unusual plants. Unlike many hybrid cactus, Lloyd's hedgehog is not always sterile, but rather is often functionally bisexual, able backcross with both of its parents. It has the clearest orange flowers of all of the hedgehog species. Mature fruit are purple-maroon to brick red.

DESIGN SUGGESTIONS

Try Lloyd's hedgehog alongside drought-tolerant, low-growing perennials such as Angelita daisy (*Tetranueris acaulis*), and damianita daisy (*Chrysactinia neomexicana*).

CULTIVATION

Has an affinity with limestone soils. Consider adding dolomitic limestone to potting soil mixes.

NOTABLE VARIETIES, FORMS, AND SUBSPECIES

The Jarilla Mountains in southeastern New Mexico are to home to a hybrid swarm with fabulous flowers in yellow, orange, red, and peach with stunning bicolor combinations.

A STOCKY LLOYD'S HEDGEHOG PUTS ON AN APRIL SHOW IN A DISPLAY GARDEN AT BACH'S CACTUS NURSERY IN TUCSON.

ECHINOCEREUS RUSSANTHUS SUBSP. *WEEDINII* WITH OVER 2 DOZEN BLOSSOMS ON THE SIDES OF ITS STEMS IN A SANTA FE, NEW MEXICO, ROCK GARDEN.

Growing at high elevations in the Davis Mountains, this cold-hardy, yellow-spined hedgehog is a great alternative to the golden hedgehog for those who live in colder climate zones.

Echinocereus russanthus subsp. *weedinii*
(Also sold as *Echinocereus viridiflorus* var. *weedinii*)

green-flowered pitaya; green-flowering torch cactus

NATIVE HABITAT	MATURE SIZE	HARDINESS	FLOWERING SEASON
Davis Mountains, west Texas	5–9 inches (13–23 cm) high, forming clumps up to 8–15 inches (20–38 cm) across	Zone 6	Mid- to late spring

► Despite its name, green-flowered pitaya is known for its shaggy golden spines and unusual brown-yellow flowers that are often clustered on the sides of the stems. The flowers are the same shade as some old-fashioned garden mums, and for that reason they remind me of autumn. In cultivation, this cactus is among the first hedgehogs to bloom. While its flowers are small, they are abundant. Green-flowered pitaya makes an excellent garden plant, thanks to its colorful spination, which gives it year-round interest. This plant is very rare in cultivation but well worth seeking out.

DESIGN SUGGESTIONS
Cluster this plant among boulders or rockwork

CULTIVATION
Prefers to have constricted roots; do not overpot. Best planted in situation with very fast draining soil where the plant can be left undisturbed for several years.

PETER BESTE'S EL PASO GARDEN
BRIMS WITH PAINTERLY SWATHES OF
FIERY CLARET CUP CACTUS
AND MEXICAN GOLD POPPIES.

BLOOMING AMIDST NATIVE
GRASSES AT WHITE
SANDS NATIONAL MONUMENT.

CLARET CUP MIXES WITH SAGE, PENSTEMON, NATIVE GRASSES,
AND FOUR O'CLOCKS IN A COLORADO ROCK GARDEN.

The claret cups are the most well-studied group of hedgehog cactus, but also the most controversial. In the past, many claret cup hedgehogs were considered forms of *Echinocereus triglochidiatus* (*E. coccineus* being one example) but are now classified as independent species. For gardening purposes, several of the claret cup-type hedgehogs are excellent and sought after for their cold hardiness, exceptional forms, and flowers. Here, I cover the three claret cups I consider most garden worthy.

THE HEAVYWEIGHT CHAMPION OF CLARET CUPS, 'WHITE SANDS STRAIN', BLOOMING AT WHITE SANDS NATIONAL MONUMENT.

'WHITE SANDS STRAIN' CLARET CUP IN A GARDEN SETTING, GROWING ALONGSIDE BUCKWHEAT AND YUCCA.

Charming Claret Cups

Echinocereus triglochidiatus 'White Sands Strain'
(Also sold as *Echinocereus triglochidiatus* var. *gonacanthus*)

White Sands claret cup hedgehog

The giant of the hedgehogs, White Sands claret cup is known for its speedy growth, cold hardiness, sparse thorns, and deep red flowers.

NATIVE HABITAT	MATURE SIZE	HARDINESS	FLOWERING SEASON
White Sands National Monument and nearby portions of south-central New Mexico	2–3 feet (0.6–0.9 m) high and 2–6 feet (0.6 m–1.8 m) across	Zone 5	Mid- to late spring

► Muscular stems with widely spaced, stout thorns make White Sands claret cup's medium-green flesh more visible. Its stems grow more upright than other hedgehogs and the scarlet-red flowers and green flesh combine for a very attractive color contrast. In winter, the stems of White Sands claret cup turn reddish-purple. A medium-sized plant can produce over 50 flowers that bloom for several weeks. The flowers are followed by fruit that turns orange when ripe. The growth of the White Sands claret cup is vigorous. Santa Fe plantsman David Salman grew a 15-inch-tall, multi-stemmed, freely blooming plant in only 7 years from seed. In their native habitat, White Sands claret cups can be gargantuan with some individuals forming clumps over 6 feet across.

WHITE SANDS CLARET CUP BLOOMING IN HABITAT AT WHITE SANDS NATIONAL MONUMENT IN NEW MEXICO.

CULINARY VALUE
Strawberry-flavored fruit

DESIGN SUGGESTIONS
The deep-red flowers of the claret cup look smashing paired with gold- or yellow-flowered drought-tolerant perennials. Try Kannah Creek buckwheat (*Eriogonum umbellatum* var. *aureum* 'Psdowns' [Kannah Creek]; 'Comanche Campfire' evening primrose (*Oenothera macrocarpa* 'Comanche Campfire'); and paper flower (*Psilostrophe tagetina*).

CULTIVATION
Because 'White Sands Strain' is found growing at the base of gypsum sand dunes among grasses in a sandy/clay soil mix, adding a bit of gypsum to your soil mix may give the plant a boost. Gypsum soil amendments loosen up tight clay soils.

Echinocerus triglochidiatus subsp. *mojavensis* forma *inermis*
(Also sold as *Echinocereus inermis*; *Echinocereus triglochidiatus*
var. *inermis*; *Echinocereus coccineus* var. *inermis*)

spineless hedgehog

If you want an *uber* cold-hardy spineless hedgehog with interesting medium-green skin and scarlet red flowers, look no further.

NATIVE HABITAT

The La Sal Mountains and Book Cliffs along the Utah-Colorado border at elevations from 5000–7200 feet (1500–2160 m)

MATURE SIZE

8–31 inches (20–80 cm) high and 12–20 inches (30–51 cm) wide

HARDINESS

Zone 5

FLOWERING SEASON

Midspring to early summer

► Prized by cactus enthusiasts and rock gardeners, the spineless hedgehog grows in a small area on both sides of the Utah-Colorado border in high mountain habitats. It is listed as an endangered species in the wild, but cultivated specimens grown from seed are readily available in the nursery trade. Smaller than other hedgehogs, it still can form clusters of up to 50 stems. In habitat, it will grow next to other claret cup cactus plants with thorns, and therefore has been taxonomically downgraded from a variety to a form; this tweak to the botanical name is not yet reflected in most nursery labeling and it is most often known by *Echinocereus inermis* in the cactus trade.

CULINARY VALUE

Edible fruit

DESIGN SUGGESTIONS

Cluster with other cactus or grow in a pot where its mostly bald nature can be appreciated. Yellow flowers, such as Mexican gold poppy (*Eschscholtzia mexicana*), look stunning next to its scarlet blooms.

CULTIVATION

Same as *Echinocereus triglochidiatus* 'White Sands Strain'

SPINELESS HEDGEHOG BLOOMING IN A NEW MEXICO ROCK GARDEN NEXT TO PERENNIALS AND OTHER ACCENT PLANTS.

Its small size, super cold hardiness, and green flowers, which are strongly scented of lemons, make the green-flowered hedgehog very desirable.

Echinocereus viridiflorus
(Also sold as *Echinocereus chloranthus* var. *cylindricus*)

green-flowered hedgehog; nylon hedgehog

NATIVE HABITAT

South Dakota, Colorado, and New Mexico, where it is found growing at altitudes up to 8900 feet (2670 m), as well as in Wyoming, Kansas, and west Texas

MATURE SIZE

3–12 inches (8–30 cm) tall and 2–24 inches (5–60 cm) across

HARDINESS

Zone 4b

FLOWERING SEASON

Mid- to late spring

▶ This dwarf has alluring flowers that nearly glow chartreuse. It produces prodigious blooms over a fairly long season. In the fall, it shrivels up until its stems are flush with the ground. The stems and ribs are often purple-red and in some populations the spines are a brightly colored mix of mahogany, red, and white. Green-flowered hedgehog occupies the most northerly range—clear into South Dakota—of any plant in the *Echinocereus* genus. Older plants can grow up to a dozen branches.

DESIGN SUGGESTIONS

Exceptional in trough and rock gardens, especially growing with other small plants

CULTIVATION

So long as its roots are kept reasonably dry, green-flowered hedgehog can withstand subzero temperatures and deep snow cover for prolonged periods. If overwintered indoors, do so in an unheated space.

NOTABLE VARIETIES, FORMS, AND SUBSPECIES

Subspecies *correllii* is a taller, more erect plant with horizontal bands of spines that are shades of green, yellow, and white.

THE ALLURING GREEN-YELLOW BLOOMS OF THE GREEN-FLOWERED HEDGEHOG STAND OUT IN THIS COLORADO ROCK GARDEN PLANTING.

A SOLITARY ROCK-GARDEN BEEHIVE
JUST CRACKING BUD.

MISSOURI FOXTAIL CACTUS BLOOMING IN THE
KELAIDIS GARDEN IN COLORADO.

▶ Small, ball-shaped, and often clustering, the cactus that make up this group (known as both *Escobaria* and *Coryphantha*) offer high impact for their size, and are generally very cold hardy. Many have fragrant flowers and some have edible fruit. Most of the plants in this genus will fit nicely into either a rock garden or an unirrigated short-grass prairie setting. There are around 20 species in this group; I've chosen five that I consider most garden worthy.

There is much confusion regarding the name of the genus that beehive cactus belong to. Edward Anderson's *The Cactus Family* uses the genus *Escobaria* to describe them, but *Flora of North America* does not, and continues to call some of the plants in the genus *Coryphantha*. As much as possible, I've listed the plants under their current accepted name and have included other names you might find the plant listed under in nursery descriptions under the designation "also sold as."

MISSOURI FOXTAIL CACTUS NESTLED INTO
A NATURALISTIC PRAIRIE PLANTING.

HOT PINK AND HIGHLY PERFUMED, THE BEEHIVE CACTUS FLOWERS
MAKE IT AN IRRESISTIBLE GARDEN ADDITION.

Beehive Brilliance

Escobaria missouriensis
(Also sold as *Neobesseya missouriensis*)

Missouri foxtail cactus; Missouri pincushion

Excellent for planting in a naturalistic prairie-themed garden among native grasses and wildflowers. Equally handsome in a pot, Missouri foxtail cactus has remarkable cold tolerance with winter interest to boot.

NATIVE HABITAT

Arizona to North Dakota, Texas, Kansas, New Mexico, and Idaho; Coahuila and Nuevo León, Mexico

MATURE SIZE

1–3 inches (2.5–7.6 cm) high and 12 inches (30 cm) across

HARDINESS

Zone 3 to 6, depending on the plant's origin

FLOWERING SEASON

Midspring to early summer

*Escobaria missouriensis
Mont. Co. KS SB*

A STRIKING CONTAINER PLANTING OF MISSOURI FOXTAIL CACTUS IN THE COLLECTION OF COLORADO HORTICULTURIST PANAYOTI KELAIDIS.

► The Missouri foxtail cactus's body is unusually deep green, providing good contrast to the yellow-pink flowers which grace its crown. Its native habitat encompasses a wide range, making it quite adaptable to different planting conditions. It is found growing in rocky loam soils in oak woodlands as well as on exposed short-grass prairie. The cactus is ball-shaped and often branches, forming a clump, although some specimens remain solitary. It grows from short taproots; in winter the rounded heads may retreat to near soil level giving it a flattop appearance. The orange to scarlet fruit is handsome and persists on the plant through winter, adding extra interest. The fruit is borne down between the tubercles (little cone-shaped protrusions that extend out from the plant's body) and below the spines, making it hard to harvest without tweezers.

CULINARY VALUE
Edible fruit

DESIGN SUGGESTIONS
One of the best cactus to slip into a short-grass meadow planting among other grasses. Try it with other meadow-adapted cactus such as *Opuntia polyacantha* and *Escobaria vivipara*.

CULTIVATION
Although it is tolerant of a variety of soils, keep the roots as dry as possible in winter.

Escobaria orcutti var. *koenigii*

Koenig's snowball, snowball beehive

The body of Koenig's snowball is encased in a nearly pure-white mesh of spines. A ring of delicate salmon-colored flowers encircles its top, making this Denver-hardy plant a popular choice for rock-gardeners.

NATIVE HABITAT

Southeastern Arizona and southwestern New Mexico

MATURE SIZE

6 inches (15 cm) tall and 10 inches (25 cm) wide

HARDINESS

Zone 5

FLOWERING SEASON

Mid- to late spring

▶ Truly a snowball-colored plant, the dense white spination of Koenig's snowball brands it as garden worthy. Interesting salmon-colored flowers and a clumping habit make for a tidy little plant. After flowering, it produces small green fruit. Koenig's snowball hails from high-elevation crevices in the limestone slopes of Arizona and New Mexico, giving it good cold tolerance. Given time, it will form a cluster of over 20 stems.

DESIGN SUGGESTIONS

Excellent in a trough garden that mimics its rocky natural habitat. Small buckwheat species (*Eriogonum* species) and other cushion-type rock garden plants will look good beside it.

CULTIVATION

Likes exceptionally well-drained soils. If planting in the ground, try situating it on mounds; otherwise, plant in a shallow bowl in a fast-draining cactus mix.

KOENIG'S SNOWBALL COMING INTO BLOOM IN A HIGH-ELEVATION ROCK GARDEN.

LEE'S DWARF SNOWBALL IN A NEW MEXICO ROCK GARDEN.

Its diminutive size and tightly knit thatch of white spines makes Lee's dwarf snowball desirable in small rock gardens.

Escobaria sneedii subsp. *leei*
(Also sold as *Escobaria leei; Coryphantha sneedii* subsp. *leei*)

Lee's dwarf snowball; Lee's pincushion

NATIVE HABITAT	MATURE SIZE	HARDINESS	FLOWERING SEASON
Guadalupe Mountains, Texas	0.5–2 inches (1.3–5.1 cm) high by 6–12 inches (15–30 cm) across	Zone 4	Mid- to late spring

► Some believe that Lee's dwarf snowball is a freak genetic variety of Sneed's pincushion. In habitat, it produces up to 300 1/2-inch-wide (1.3 cm) stems that form dense mounds. It grows in limestone fissures with very quick drainage. In cultivation, it will typically be much smaller, on the order of 20–40 snow-white, ball-shaped stems. It is listed as threatened under the U.S. Endangered Species Act, so take care to buy the plant only from reputable dealers who have grown it from seed. The flowers are salmon-pink.

DESIGN SUGGESTIONS

This might be the best cactus of all for planting in the nooks and pockets of rock retaining walls; it is equally handsome in hypertufa containers.

CULTIVATION

Although the trade of wild plants is prohibited, Lee's dwarf snowball is easy to propagate from stem cuttings. Grow it in coarse, well-drained soil. Plant Lee's snowball on south or west exposures where you can wedge it between rocks.

Escobaria sneedii subsp. *sneedii*
(Also sold as *Coryphantha sneedii var. sneedii*)

Sneed's pincushion cactus

Its miniature size, along with a profusion of ball-shaped white-spined stems, make Sneed's pincushion interesting in small containers or rock planters.

NATIVE HABITAT

A small portion of Texas, and one county in New Mexico. Sneed's pincushion is most prolific in the limestone substrates of the Franklin Mountains near El Paso, Texas.

MATURE SIZE

0.6 to 3.5 inches (1.5–9 cm) high and clumps up to 24 inches (60 cm) across

HARDINESS

Zone 5

FLOWERING SEASON

Early spring to early summer, sometimes blooming again following summer rains

▶ Sneed's pincushion grows in limestone slopes where its roots find purchase in tiny fissures. The stems are so covered in a white web of spines as to mostly obscure the plant's flesh. Its stems are quite small and range in diameter from a marble-sized 5/8 inch (1.5 cm) to tennis-ball scale, 3 inches (7.6 cm) across. In the steep rocky terrain that is its habitat, the plant produces a dense series of cascading stems (up to 50!) that give the plant a lacy, trailing aspect. Sneed's pincushion has light pink to mauve flowers that bloom near the plant's crown. Only buy this plant from trusted nurseries that grow it from seed. The plant's limited range makes it a likely target for poaching. It is listed as endangered in the U.S. Endangered Species Act.

DESIGN SUGGESTIONS

Excellent growing from a dry-stacked retaining wall, or equally impressive trailing out of a rustic container.

CULTIVATION

Take care to shield the Sneed's pincushion from excess rain during the spring and fall. Sneed's pincushion can be propagated from stem cuttings.

AN ELEGANT POTTED SPECIMEN OF SNEED'S PINCUSHION SURROUNDED BY A YELLOW-FLOWERED BUCKWHEAT.

Escobaria vivipara
(Also sold as *Coryphantha vivipara*)

beehive cactus; spiny star

Highly fragrant hot-pink flowers, exceptionally tasty fruit, Canadian cold tolerance, and a tidy rounded form make the beehive cactus a must-have.

NATIVE HABITAT

A wide range from northern Mexico, through the Great Plains and into southern Canada

MATURE SIZE

Up to 4–6 inches (10–15 cm) tall and 8–20 inches (20–51 cm) wide

HARDINESS

Zone 4b

FLOWERING SEASON

Late spring to early summer, with a possible repeat bloom after heavy summer rains

▶ In the wild, the beehive's range extends from northern Mexico to southern Canada, making it one of the most adapted species to both cold and heat. It is found growing in a wide range of soil types and can grow in the open among grasses or beneath shrubs. In the garden, its handsome mounding hemispherical form (it can be solitary, but older plants usually branch), and highly fragrant flowers distinguish the beehive cactus. Its flowers are often bright pink with white throats. During winter, the stems may shrink and retreat partway under ground.

CULINARY VALUE

The green- and purple-tinged fruit has a wonderful strawberry-kiwi flavor and was a prized food plant among the Lakota tribe on the Great Plains.

DESIGN SUGGESTIONS

Incorporate in naturalistic meadow plantings with grama grasses, Indian paintbrush (*Castilleja* species), and plains prickly pear (*Opuntia polyacantha*).

CULTIVATION

Will tolerate many weeks or even months of snow cover, provided that the soil is suitably well drained around the roots.

NOTABLE VARIETIES, FORMS, AND SUBSPECIES

A large multi-headed and thick-spined plant form from southern Arizona, *Escobaria vivipara* var. *bisbeeana*, known as the Bisbee spiny star, is a much sought-after specimen for collectors. *E. vivipara* var. *rosea* has flowers that are darker pink without the typical white throat of the straight species.

ESCOBARIA VIVIPARA VAR. *ROSEA* BLOOMING IN EARLY JUNE IN THE BARNETT GARDEN, PUEBLO, COLORADO.

The best-known psychoactive cactus, peyote is surprisingly easy to grow and makes handsome—if slightly grotesque—spineless clumps that are nice curiosities in a collection.

A LARGE PEYOTE CLUMP IN HABITAT, GROWING IN THE LIGHT SHADE OF A CREOSOTE BUSH.

Lophophora williamsii

peyote, diabolic root, divine cactus, dry whiskey, mescal button, white mule

NATIVE HABITAT

Chihuahuan Desert and Tamaulipan thornscrub and limestone soils along the Texas-Mexico border

MATURE SIZE

2–4 inches (5.1–10 cm) high and clumps up to 12 inches (30 cm) wide

HARDINESS

Zone 8

FLOWERING SEASON

Early spring through early autumn

► Peyote is fat, spineless, and nearly flush with the ground. Their rounded, blue-green, Jabba-the-Huttesque appearance makes them an interesting addition to collections. Over time, a single head can mound into a large lumpy colony attractive to those with a taste for corpulent plants. Certainly, some peyote gardeners have motives beyond ornamental horticulture. Although I'm not advocating consumption, the plant can be propagated (and harvested) by cutting off the top of the body and letting the root re-sprout. Because peyote contains the alkaloid mescaline, consuming the dried tops of the plant (buttons) can produce powerful hallucinations that are usually preceded by nausea. Below ground, a parsnip-shaped taproot stores moisture and carbohydrates. In nature, they usually hunker below sparsely leaved shrubs; in cultivation, they will take partial sunlight and can even be grown indoors on a bright windowsill. The flowers are rather unremarkable—small and light pink—but produced regularly during the warm season. In the United States, both federal and state laws govern the possession of peyote, so you should familiarize yourself with the laws regarding peyote cultivation and use in your area.

DESIGN SUGGESTIONS

Peyote is a very handsome and user-friendly (pun intended) plant for a dish garden. Because of its thornless nature, you can use it in a sensory planting the same way you might employ living stones (*Lithops* species).

CULTIVATION

To account for its taproot, plant peyote in a deeper than normal pot. It is easy to grow from seed, and because the flowers are self-fertile, once you have one plant flowering it will produce ample seed.

AN ARTFULLY POTTED PINCUSHION (*MAMMILLARIA KARWINSKIANA*) READY FOR JUDGING AT A CACTUS AND SUCCULENT SHOW.

Since the beginning of horticultural exploration in the Americas, botanists and collectors have fawned over genus *Mammillaria*. Its 171 some-odd recognized species have been extensively studied, traded, admired, and smuggled out of the wild. Some of this smuggling is because of their compact size and portability, but that doesn't explain all of their allure. Mammillarias are universally loved for their concentric rings of flowers that come in nearly every shade of the rainbow, their densely woven spines, and their little chili-pepper-shaped fruit that is often tasty. The seed collecting and locality documentation of American nurseryman Steve Brack has helped secure a supply of domestic seed-grown plants that, at least to some extent, takes pressure off of the plants in the wild. Because the supply of seed-grown plants is plentiful, avoid buying wild-collected specimens in order to preserve the range of this magnificent genus of cactus.

AN EXPERTLY CURATED MASS PLANTING OF TWIN-SPINED PINCUSHION PLANTS IN A
LAVA ROCK GARDEN AT THE HUNTINGTON BOTANICAL GARDENS IN CALIFORNIA.

A VENERABLE POTTED PINCUSHION GRACES
A BRICK PATIO IN A TUCSON GARDEN.

Hooked on Pincushions

Its yellow flowers smell exactly like its namesake cleaning product.

Mammillaria baumii

Lemon Pledge–scented pincushion

NATIVE HABITAT

Tamaulipas, Mexico, where it grows under shrubs

MATURE SIZE

3–4 inches (7.6–10 cm) tall, forming clusters to 6 inches (15 cm) wide

HARDINESS

Zone 9a (25° F or 4° C)

FLOWERING SEASON

Late spring through early summer

► Fuzzy white hairs nearly obscure the stems of the Lemon Pledge–scented pincushion. Individual stems are 2–3 inches high (5.1–7.6 cm) and 3–6 inches (7.6–15 cm) in diameter. The plant is a generous bloomer and older plants may send out more than 40 flowers at the same time. Blindfolded, you would swear the scent was something concocted in a household products lab, but no, it is a natural perfume. Although the number-one reason to grow this pincushion might be the fragrance of the flowers, its compact size, handsome white spines, and clumping nature also recommend it. It will flower in 3 to 4 years if grown by seed.

DESIGN SUGGESTIONS

I prefer to place this plant, potted, on a bench near a south-facing doorway, where one can easily smell the flowers when it is blooming.

CULTIVATION

Although in the wild it grows beneath shrubs, this easy-to-grow species prefers bright light and high temperatures in cultivation. The stronger light will promote dense spine development. Over the years, it will freely clump and form dense clusters of stems.

LEMON PLEDGE–SCENTED PINCUSHION POTTED IN A CHOCOLATE-BROWN TERRA COTTA CONTAINER.

SNOWBALL PINCUSHION COMING INTO PEPPERMINT-STRIPED BLOOM IN SPRING.

With densely crosshatched pure-white spines and delicate peppermint-pink-striped flowers, the snowball pincushion is the most feminine-looking cactus in the pincushion family.

Mammillaria candida
(Also sold as *Mammilloydia candida*)

snowball pincushion

NATIVE HABITAT

Widespread in the northeastern Mexican states of Coahuila, Nuevo León, San Luis Potosí, and Tamaulipas.

MATURE SIZE

12 inches (30 cm) high with stems 5–6 inches (13–15 cm) in diameter

HARDINESS

Zone 9a

FLOWERING SEASON

Late spring to early summer

► Snowball cactus can be solitary or clustering. Its form, especially when the plant is young, is almost perfectly spherical—like a snowball. Although the spines are usually white, some plants sport a flush of pink at their crowns. Like most pincushions, its flowers bloom in concentric circular patterns around each stem tip, like the rings around Saturn. Some taxonomists have moved the snowball cactus into its own genus, *Mammilloydia*, but it is typically found in nurseries labeled as *Mammillaria*.

DESIGN SUGGESTIONS

The pastel white and pink color of the snowball cactus cries out for a powder-blue succulent companion plant. Consider planting it with *Yucca nana* or *Agave parryi*.

CULTIVATION

The snowball cactus needs extra-good drainage. See Steve Plath's Ultra-Drain in the "Cactus Soil Mixes for Containers" section. If grown in full sun, its pure-white stems will grow so densely as to completely obscure the stem.

Mammillaria canelensis

Sierra Canelo pincushion

If you become tired of white pincushions with pink flowers, *Mammillaria canelensis* provides an excellent reprieve. Its distinctive orange-yellow spines and yellow flowers, set against cotton-white wool, combine in a unique pincushion.

NATIVE HABITAT

Mountains in Chihuahua and southeast Sonora, Mexico, at elevations between 5500 and 6500 feet (1700–2000 m)

MATURE SIZE

2–5 inches (5.1–13 cm) tall and 4–5 inches (10–13 cm) acrosswide

HARDINESS

Zone 8

FLOWERING SEASON

Mid- to late spring

► *Mammillaria canelensis* grows from a solitary stem, which eventually can offset new branches at the base, perhaps after 8 to 10 years. However, it is rare to see a specimen in a botanical collection with more than one stem. One of the most attractive features of this plant are the woolly white tufts that resemble snow, in the depressions between the tubercles. They contrast nicely with its yellow spines and flowers. It should be noted that some *M. canelensis* individuals bloom hot pink, although yellow-flowered plants are more common in the trade. This is a nice compact plant that will look equally stunning in a pot or in the ground. Along with several other *Mammillaria* species, taxonomists have recently reclassified *M. canelensis* as *M. standleyi*, but I'm listing it as *M. canelensis* because the plants in the nursery trade are labeled as such and will look like the plant pictured here.

CULINARY VALUE
Edible fruit

DESIGN SUGGESTIONS

Excellent in a small pot on a bench as part of a collection of pincushions. Otherwise, consider planting several underneath the lacy foliage canopy of a desert tree such as a palo verde or mesquite tree.

CULTIVATION

In the hottest low desert climates, provide afternoon shade.

SIERRA CANELO PINCUSHION GROWING BENEATH A PALO VERDE TREE AT TUCSON BOTANICAL GARDENS.

Mammillaria dioica

California fishhook cactus

With mahogany spines and peppermint-fluted flowers, the California fishhook is a dark-spined, pincushion-type cactus that is excellent for both hot inland and seaside Mediterranean conditions.

NATIVE HABITAT	MATURE SIZE	HARDINESS	FLOWERING SEASON
California and Baja California, Mexico	12 inches (30 cm) high and to 8 inches (20 cm) across	Zone 9b	Early spring to midspring

► California fishhook cactus could be said to have a split personality. It thrives in desert and coastal climates. In fact, next to the compass barrel, it may have the highest heat tolerance (148° F—64.5° C—after acclimation!) of any cactus. Strangely, the plant is equally happy in cooler conditions near the coast; some of the California fishhook's native range is very close to the Pacific Ocean. It still needs excellent drainage however, and is as prone to collapse from overwatering as many in the genus. In contrast with some in its genus, its fishhook-like spines are an attractive brownish-red. The flowers have red candy stripes on the backs of their petals but are otherwise whitish-pink or occasionally yellowish-white. The plants will sometimes branch a good distance up the stems. California fishhook cactus is enormously variable over its huge range. The plants I'm describing are typical of the more northern forms.

CULINARY VALUE
Tasty strawberry-flavored fruit

DESIGN SUGGESTIONS
Excellent in coastal gardens alongside native plants such as San Diego sunflower (*Viguiera deltoidea*) and chalk dudleya (*Dudleya brittoniana*)

CULTIVATION
Well-drained soil, with either light shade or full sun. California fishhook grows from the roasting desert to the foggy coast and handles either situation.

CALIFORNIA FISHHOOK CACTUS IN HABITAT NEAR ENSENADA, BAJA CALIFORNIA NORTE, MEXICO.

Long, snowy-white spines and a large, uniform clustering habit make twin-spined mammillaria an excellent garden choice.

Mammillaria geminispina

twin-spined cactus

NATIVE HABITAT

Hildalgo, Querétaro, and San Luis Potosí, Mexico

MATURE SIZE

To 8 inches (20 cm) high and clumps to 16 inches (40 cm) wide

HARDINESS

Zone 9

FLOWERING SEASON

Early spring to midspring, and sometimes early autumn in cultivation

► Twin-spined cactus is one of the most popular and oldest mammillarias in cultivation. A specimen was brought to London over 170 years ago, and by 1940, large plants were established in lava-rock mulched beds at the Huntington Botanical Gardens in San Marino, California. As its name suggests, the twin-spined cactus has two different spine types: long, white, central spines extend up to 2 inches beyond the body of the plant, while shorter, radial spines cling more closely to the stems. Flowers are deep pink to carmine red and are produced in circles near the tip of the stems. The flowers are about 1/3 inch (7 mm) in diameter.

CULINARY VALUE

Edible fruit with crunchy black seeds

DESIGN SUGGESTIONS

For a surreal, high-contrast effect, plant several and mulch with a dark colored gravel mulch.

CULTIVATION

One of the more forgiving pincushions except when it comes to cold; plant twin-spined cactus in a location where the temperature doesn't drop below 20° F (6.5° C) or stay below freezing for more than 24 hours.

NOTABLE VARIETIES, FORMS, AND SUBSPECIES

Mammillaria geminispina subsp. *leucocentra* has shorter spines and prominent rings of white wool around the tips of the plant.

AN ARMY OF TWIN-
SPINED CACTUS MARCH
ACROSS A SLOPE
MULCHED WITH PUMICE
AT THE HUNTINGTON
BOTANICAL GARDEN IN
CALIFORNIA.

FISHHOOK
PINCUSHION WITH
FLOWERS READY
TO OPEN IN A NEW
MEXICO GARDEN.

An adaptable pincushion with chestnut-colored hooked spines and pink flowers followed by a tasty fruit.

Mammillaria grahamii

fishhook pincushion; Graham fishhook

NATIVE HABITAT

California east to Texas, and the Mexican states of Sonora and Chihuahua

MATURE SIZE

3–8 inches (7.6–20 cm) tall and 3–4 inches (7.6–10 cm) wide

HARDINESS

Zone 8

FLOWERING SEASON

Midspring (sometimes); mid- to late summer

Fishhook pincushion can be either solitary or clumping, and has one of the largest native ranges of any pincushion cactus in North America. It is adaptable to a variety of growing conditions. You might find it clustered at the base of a cholla cactus or foothills palo verde tree in the low desert, or growing with blue grama grass and oaks at higher elevations. Fishhook pincushion flowers in rings on its crown after heavy rains in the warm season and will sometimes flower in midspring as well. Its flowers range from a pale pink to lavender-pink. The small fishhook spines sometimes snag unaware birds and lizards.

CULINARY VALUE

Exceptionally tasty sweet-acid, club-shaped fruit that resemble tiny chili peppers

DESIGN SUGGESTIONS

Excellent clustered around the base of arid climate trees or combined with other cactus species, particularly barrel cactus

CULTIVATION

Plant in very fast-draining soil. If potting, use Steve Plath's Ultra Drain. Put in full sun in northern climates; in low deserts, it will tolerate some shade. Do not overpot and only transplant every 4 years.

Mammillaria guelzowiana

big pink pincushion

With the largest flowers of any mammillaria, these big, 3-inch-wide beauties have a clove-like scent. To see the big pink pincushion in bloom is to want one.

NATIVE HABITAT	**MATURE SIZE**	**HARDINESS**	**FLOWERING SEASON**
Durango, Mexico	4–6 inches (10–15 cm) high and up to 6 inches (15 cm) across wide	Zone 9b	Early spring to midspring

► The plant is covered in wavy, hairlike white spines. The stems mound on top of each other. Although big pink pincushion is a popular plant, it is not the easiest plant to grow—it demands perfect drainage, dislikes being repotted, and prefers some protection from harsh summer sunlight. However, once you have it potted in the right conditions, it doesn't ask a lot from you. Its pink flowers can completely obscure the plant's stems in the spring and the spicy fragrance is wonderful. The huge, smelly flowers more than make up for the cultural challenges of growing big pink pincushion.

CULINARY VALUE
Edible fruit

DESIGN SUGGESTIONS
Pot in an ornamental container that can be moved to a prime garden position once the flowering starts. Because of the intensity of the pink flowers, it looks particularly striking in pots with cobalt blue glazes.

CULTIVATION
This pincushion is a bit of a challenge to grow and requires perfect drainage. Grow in a very well-drained, gritty soil mix (See Steve Plath's Ultra-Drain in the "Cactus Soil Mixes for Containers" section), grow in a shallow pot and only transplant when the big pink pincushion is literally busting out of its container.

BIG PINK PUTTING ON A SHOW IN A TALAVERA POT IN THE AUTHOR'S GARDEN.

Mammillaria hahniana
old lady cactus

Striking for its long white hairs, which can densely cloak the plant's body, old lady cactus produces concentric rings of dark pink flowers on the stems. It is a popular plant with beginning and expert cactus gardeners alike.

NATIVE HABITAT

Guanajuato, Tamaulipas and Querértaro, Mexico, at between 2500 and 7200 feet (750–2.200 m)

MATURE SIZE

Mounding to 8 inches (20 cm) high and 10 inches (25 cm) across

HARDINESS

Zone 9

FLOWERING SEASON

Early spring to midspring

► Because the length and thickness of the white hairs on individual plants vary, old lady cactus is a species best selected in person rather than ordering through the mail. Generally, specimens with the longest hairy spines are most desirable. Some individuals have short, white spines. The body of old lady cactus is squat and tends to cluster.

DESIGN SUGGESTIONS

Best in a low, wide bowl on a bench or table where the form of the plant can be admired at eye-level

CULTIVATION

Like other pincushions, it needs excellent drainage

NOTABLE VARIETIES, FORMS, AND SUBSPECIES

Subspecies *woodsii* has dark central spines and is not as hairy as the straight species.

A MATURE OLD LADY CACTUS POTTED FOR SHOW AT B & B CACTUS FARM IN TUCSON, ARIZONA.

A HANDSOME SPECIMEN PLANTED IN THE GROUND AT TUCSON BOTANICAL GARDENS.

Apple-sized, pure-white heads with close-cropped spines and deep purple-magenta flowers make *Mammillaria klissingiana* a choice garden plant.

Mammillaria klissingiana

NATIVE HABITAT

Tamaulipas, Nuevo León, and San Luis Potosí, Mexico, where it grows on limestone cliffs, sometimes at the base of shrubs

MATURE SIZE

6–10 inches (15–25 cm) tall and clumps to 16 inches (40 cm) across

HARDINESS

Zone 9b

FLOWERING SEASON

Late spring to early summer

► A clumping plant with snow-colored spines that completely mask the body, *Mammillaria klissingiana* is less common than other similar pincushions such as twin-spined cactus (*M. geminispina*), but it is equally deserving of recognition. Like twin-spined pincushion, it will form a very large mound, but without the long central spines of twin-spined pincushion. *Mammillaria klissingiana* has a tidier, less-shaggy appearance.

DESIGN SUGGESTIONS

This is another handsome plant to cluster below native shrubs such as creosote bush (*Larrea tridentata*) or other similar shrubs. It is also excellent in a large, shallow bowl.

CULTIVATION

A little slower-growing than other similar pincushions; make sure that soil is exceptionally well drained and that the plant is not placed in too large a pot (overpotted). It is a plant that will take full sun when properly acclimatized, as its dense white spines suggest.

With dense, woolly stems, large white-pink flowers, and a compact mounding habit, woolly flattop is an irresistible pincushion to any collector. Perhaps its most unique feature is its habit of bearing fruit and flowers simultaneously.

Mammillaria lenta

woolly flattop pincushion

NATIVE HABITAT	**MATURE SIZE**	**HARDINESS**	**FLOWERING SEASON**
Coahuila, Mexico, at elevations between 2950 and 4600 feet (900–1400 m)	0.5–1 inch (1.3–2.5 cm) high and forming clumps to 16 inches (40 cm) across	Zone 9	Early to late spring

► This low and slow-growing pincushion is known to bring home blue ribbons at cactus and succulent shows even against competition from larger, flashier species (such as *Mammillaria geminispina*). It has the diminutive look of a true rock garden plant, and in its native range it finds purchase between cracks in limestone boulders. Its flowers are a pleasing white with pink pin-striping, and the red club-shaped fruit persists side-by-side with the flowers. With patience, one can grow an eye-catching clump with many heads suitable for a pincushion smackdown.

CULINARY VALUE
Edible fruit

DESIGN SUGGESTIONS
A broad, low bowl is ultimately the best container for the woolly flattop. It is a plant that is best seen up close, such as on a display table or bench.

CULTIVATION
In temperate climates, it needs exposure to full sunlight for compact growth and flowering; in the desert Southwest, filtered or afternoon shade is desirable during the hottest months. Needs excellent drainage and care should be taken not to overpot woolly flattop.

A FORMIDABLE WOOLLY FLATTOP PINCUSHION SPECIMEN GROWN IN FILTERED SHADE AT TUCSON BOTANICAL GARDENS.

AN OWL'S EYE PINCUSHION WITH MULTIPLE HEADS, STARING BACK AT YOU IN A ROCK GARDEN BED AT THE DESERT BOTANICAL GARDEN IN PHOENIX, ARIZONA.

Owl's eye is a relatively fast grower whose stems divide to form new heads; during this process the head of each plant strongly resembles the face of a barn owl. It forms a large, showy plant with time.

Mammillaria parkinsonii

owl's eye; owl's eye pincushion

NATIVE HABITAT
Querétaro, Mexico, at elevations between 3900 and 7900 feet (1170 and 2370 m)

MATURE SIZE
6 inches (15 cm) high and clumps 16 inches (40 cm) wide

HARDINESS
Zone 9

FLOWERING SEASON
Midspring to early summer

► One of the best pincushions for the home grower, owl's eye can form a clump of 8 to10 heads in as little as 6 years. The stems divide, rather than branch, giving it its namesake appearance. It can be planted in the ground or in a low, wide pot to great effect. Spine color can vary from plant to plant, but in the trade, the most commonly seen specimens are nearly pure white—and will remain so if grown in bright light. Its flowers are an unremarkable pale yellow; this is a plant to grow for its unusual barn-owl appearance rather than the flowers.

DESIGN SUGGESTIONS
Use this extremely showy plant near walkways or potted prominently. The owl's eye feature is most obvious when viewed from above.

CULTIVATION
Mammillaria parkinsonii will grow fast if planted in ample sun and up-potted frequently as needed.

Mammillaria plumosa

feather cactus

A pincushion friendly to the touch—its woolly spines swirl like hair around its stems, giving it a soft feathery appearance and feel.

NATIVE HABITAT

Limestone rock faces of Nuevo León, Mexico, specifically Huasteca Canyon area

MATURE SIZE

Up to 3 inches (7.6 cm) high, forming clumps up to 20 inches (51 cm) across

HARDINESS

Zone 8a

FLOWERING SEASON

Late autumn to midwinter (in cultivation)

THE BROAD-SPREADING FEATHER CACTUS FILLS UP ITS LOW CONTAINER AT TUCSON BOTANICAL GARDENS.

► This popular plant is grown for its unique form and soft spines rather than its so-so flowers. It forms pillowy cushions that are sure to draw attention from passersby. In a dish-type container, it will grow quite broadly, eventually filling a substantial pot from rim to rim. Its flowers are nothing to speak of—merely dull, whitish-yellow affairs, but the unique form is very appealing.

DESIGN SUGGESTIONS

Use feather cactus in a sensory garden or children's garden where it can be appreciated up close and touched. Feather cactus is often positioned on a table or plant stand.

CULTIVATION

Grow feather cactus in a very shallow pot and incorporate at least 50 percent grit into your soil mix.

Mammillaria senilis
(Also sold as *Mamillopsis senilis*)

old man pincushion

Old man pincushion is hairy, white-spined, and clumping. Come spring, it puts on one of the best flower displays in the genus, sending out numerous large, red flowers.

NATIVE HABITAT

High mountains in the Mexican states of Chihuahua, Durango, Jalisco, and Nayarit

MATURE SIZE

6 inches (15 cm) tall and 16 inches (40 cm) wide

HARDINESS

Zone 6

FLOWERING SEASON

Early spring to midspring

▶ Hairy white spines completely obscure old man pincushion's body. This plant comes from high up in the Sierra Madre at elevations up to 9000 feet (2800 m), where it is covered with snow in winter; as you might guess, it is very cold hardy. The flowers on old man pincushion are unusual in that they are pollinated by hummingbirds—uncommon for plants in the pincushion genus. The floristic uniqueness of this plant has botanists squabbling over whether old man pincushion belongs to the genus *Mammillaria* or *Mamillopsis*, but until gene analysis is complete, it will remain *Mammillaria*—although as often as not, it is sold as *Mamillopsis*.

DESIGN SUGGESTIONS

A very striking plant for a hummingbird garden; group it with other red-flowering plants such as firecracker penstemon (*Penstemon eatonii*).

CULTIVATION

Provide excellent drainage.

NOTABLE VARIETIES, FORMS, AND SUBSPECIES

A plant with white or chiffon-yellow flowers from Topia, Durango, Mexico, can be grown from seed from Steve Brack at Mesa Gardens.

A FLAT OF OLD MAN PINCUSHION IN FULL BLOOM AT SANTA FE GREENHOUSES IN NEW MEXICO.

Mammillaria standleyi

Standley's pincushion

Green tubercles contrast nicely with the white wool that fills the crevices near the top of its stems. Standley's pincushion is a handsome and, with time, a sizable plant for a large pot.

NATIVE HABITAT

Primarily in southern Sonora, Mexico, but also across the borders of the states of Chihuahua and Sinaloa

MATURE SIZE

6–8 inches (15–20 cm) high and forming clumps 16–24 inches (40–60 cm) wide

HARDINESS

Zone 9

FLOWERING SEASON

Early spring to midspring

► One of the most striking pincushions, Standley's pincushion is breathtaking, especially seen as a full-sized, 2-foot-wide plant in bloom. The axils (little depressions between the tubercles) are filled with white wool that resembles micro snowdrifts near the top of the stems. Its flowers are large for the genus: around 1/2 inch (12.7 mm) in diameter with purple-red petals and green stigmas.

CULINARY VALUE

Edible, tasty, club-shaped red fruit

DESIGN SUGGESTIONS

Use mature specimens in large, low pots like sentries flanking an entryway, or placed in a focal point.

CULTIVATION

In sun-intensive areas (such as Phoenix), provide some form of filtered or partial day shade.

STANDLEY'S PINCUSHION IN FULL CIRCULAR BLOOM AT THE ARIZONA-SONORA DESERT MUSEUM IN TUCSON, ARIZONA.

Mammillaria supertexta

Its short, dense web of spines makes the plant touchable, and in bloom its dark pink rings of flowers are irresistible.

NATIVE HABITAT	MATURE SIZE	HARDINESS	FLOWERING SEASON
Oaxaca, Mexico, growing from limestone cliffs	5–7 inches (13–18 cm) tall and wide	Zone 9b	Midspring to late spring

MAMMILLARIA SUPERTEXTA SIDLING UP TO A BOULDER IN A ROCK GARDEN PLANTING.

pertexta comes from Oaxaca, Mexico, it is not as cold hardy as some of the other white, short-spined pincushions such as *M. klissingiana*. *Mammillaria supertexta* grows from a single stem in habitat; in cultivation it often forms arms near the base of the plant.

CULINARY VALUE
Edible, with a sweet-tart zing

DESIGN SUGGESTIONS
Handsome in low, glazed bowls; cobalt blue glazes look particularly good next to this plant. It can also be grown in the ground near rockwork.

CULTIVATION
Plant with a high-grit, limestone-based gravel (up to 50 percent), do not overpot, and water judiciously.

► Plants sold in the trade usually have such dense, uniform spines that one can handle this plant without gloves. The spines are white, but often plants have variable spine density that gives the appearance of horizontal banding. The flowers are a rich magenta color and they appear in the concentric rings characteristic of most plants in the genus. Because *Mammillaria su-*

Super cold hardiness, jasmine-scented
flowers, and interesting spines
make the mountain ball cactus a natural
for high-elevation rock gardens.

Pediocactus simpsonii

mountain ball cactus

NATIVE HABITAT

Throughout much of the arid, high-elevation western
United States—Arizona, Colorado, Idaho, Montana,
Nevada, New Mexico, Oregon, South Dakota, and
Utah and Wyoming—between 4600 and 11,800 feet
(1400–3600 m)

MATURE SIZE

1–6 inches (2.5–15 cm)
high and 3–6 inches
(7.6–15 cm) across

HARDINESS

Zone 3

FLOWERING SEASON

Midspring to
midsummer

▶ Mountain ball cactus grows at higher elevations than any other cactus species in North America, up to 11,800 feet (3600m), making it also perhaps the continent's most cold-hardy cactus. The form of mountain ball cactus varies: it can be solitary or form clumps of up to 50 stems. In both cases, the plant contracts during the cold months. In spring it is an early bloomer and produces jasmine-scented flowers even when the night temperatures fall below freezing. Flower color is highly variable and can be white, pink, magenta, or yellow. Even mature plants (which can reach cantaloupe proportions) can be hard to locate in habitat; they are typically found on rocky substrates and are very well camouflaged with gray, red, brown, cream, and black spines. Complicating the hunt further, some mountain ball cactus remain embedded below grade during the warm season, even as they flower.

DESIGN SUGGESTIONS

A fine plant for inclusion in high-elevation rock gardens. Because the plant is small, wedge it in between boulders and in gravel beds. It can also be planted in a trough garden near an entryway where the scent of its flowers can be appreciated.

CULTIVATION

Best suited for the high-elevation Intermountain West, as it doesn't tolerate high summer humidity combined with high heat. The mountain ball cactus performs best in climates where summer nighttime temperatures regularly fall to the 50s or 60s °F (10° to 20.5° C). Use ample gravel mulch and avoid organic mulch. For gardeners in Boise, Denver, Reno, and Salt Lake City, mountain ball cactus is an excellent choice.

MOUNTAIN BALL CACTUS IN FULL SPLENDOR IN A COLORADO ROCK GARDEN.

THE ARCHITECTURAL RIDGES AND CANYONS OF *THELOCACTUS HETEROCHROMUS* APPEAL TO MANY CACTOPHILES.

▶ Although there are only 12 species of *Thelocactus*, they are among the most worthwhile and trouble-free for gardeners. All of the species in the genus are native to Northern Mexico with a couple ranging into southern Texas. The genus name is derived from the Greek *thele*, meaning nipple. All *Thelocactus* are low growers, but some are single-stemmed while others cluster. Several have wonderfully dense spines that are handsome on their own. Many of the most sought-after species have huge flowers in proportion to the size of the body of the plant—some flowers top 4 inches (10 cm) in diameter! Others have strangely articulated bodies whose form is interesting on its own. As a group, *Thelocactus* has it all—glorious spines, wonderful flowers, and interesting bodies.

THE CHIHUAHUAN SNOWBALL CACTUS STANDS OUT ON ACCOUNT OF ITS SYMMETRICAL FORM AND SPECTACULAR WHITE SPINES.

The Great Chihuahuan Nipple Cactus

A DENSELY SPINED *THELO-CACTUS BICOLOR* 'TRICOLOR'—THE MOST INTEREST-ING GLORY OF TEXAS GARDEN SELECTION— IN FULL, AUDA-CIOUS BLOOM.

Easy to grow, free-flowering, and exquisitely spined, glory of Texas is an underappreciated plant in the trade.

Thelocactus bicolor subsp. *bicolor*

glory of Texas; straw spine cactus

NATIVE HABITAT	MATURE SIZE	HARDINESS	FLOWERING SEASON
Texas and Northern Mexico, in the Chihuahuan Desert	0.6–15 inches (1.5–38 cm) high and 1–8 inches (2.5–20 cm) across	Zone 8b	Late spring to midautumn

▶ Glory of Texas is known for its huge (over 3 inches in diameter) magenta-pink flowers, which even in cultivation are reliably produced every year. The glory of Texas is a highly variable plant; spines can be yellow or red and white, and plants can be either low and squat or more upright and cylindrical. The flowers often fade to white on the outer portion of the petal as their species name *bicolor* suggests. In much of the desert Southwest glory of Texas repeat blooms several times.

DESIGN SUGGESTIONS

Excellent massed in a group of three or five plants clustered among landscape boulders and mixed with prickly pear cactus and native grasses.

CULTIVATION

Known as an easy-to-grow garden specimen, this nearly foolproof cactus is a great addition to a xeriscape garden. It more or less likes full sun exposure, can be potted or grown in the ground, and is not particular about soil so long as it is reasonably well drained.

NOTABLE VARIETIES, FORMS, AND SUBSPECIES

A golden-yellow form, labeled as *Thelocactus bicolor* subsp. *flavidispinus*, and a plant with red, yellow, and white spines, labeled 'Tricolor' (pictured here), are excellent garden plants. 'Tricolor' sports a densely thatched cone of yellow and red upward-pointing spines that makes the pink flowers pop.

An unusual sculptural form and husky interlacing spines make this Chihuahuan Desert native one of the best species for gardens.

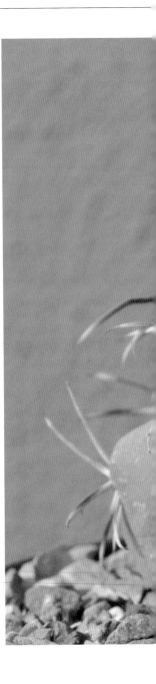

Thelocactus heterochromus

(Also sold as *Thelocactus bicolor* subsp. *heterochromus*)

NATIVE HABITAT	**MATURE SIZE**	**HARDINESS**	**FLOWERING SEASON**
Chihuahua, Coahuila, and Durango, Mexico, between the elevation of 3900 and 4600 feet (1170–1380 m)	2–3 inches (5.1–7.6 cm) high and 3–6 inches (7.6–15 cm) across	Zone 8b	Midspring to late summer

▶ Its oddly shaped, squat body makes *Thelocactus heterochromus* stand out from the rest of the genus. Its globular-shaped nipples rise up from the plant like sculptural minarets. Each round-topped nipple is topped with a sprout of thick, reddish to yellow spines, arranged like exploding fireworks. The shape of the blue-green nipples resembles fantastic structures like something that the Spanish architect Antonio Gaudi might have concocted. *Thelocactus heterochromus* typically grows as a singular plant. Its huge 4-inch diameter (10 cm) flowers are a deep magenta color.

DESIGN SUGGESTIONS

A great plant to use in clusters at the front of a cactus and succulent bed. Potted, they work well in a low dish wedged between rocks in a way that mimics their natural habitat.

CULTIVATION

Provide full, strong sun and withhold water during the cold months.

SEED-GROWN *THELOCACTUS HETEROCHROMUS* AT B & B CACTUS FARM IN TUCSON.

A POTTED
SPECIMEN OF
*THELOCACTUS
MACDOWELII*
IN FULL BLOOM.

Long crystal-white spines that resemble spun glass, and lavender-pink flowers make the Chihuahuan snowball a contender for the most beautiful plant in the genus *Thelocactus.*

Thelocactus macdowelii
(Also sold as *Thelocactus conothelos* var. *macdowelii*)

Chihuahuan snowball

NATIVE HABITAT	MATURE SIZE	HARDINESS	FLOWERING SEASON
Limestone slopes in Coahuila and Nuevo León, Mexico	2–4 inches (5.1–10 cm) high and 2–5 inches (5.1–13 cm) wide	Zone 8b	Late winter to early summer (depending on climate)

▶ Chihuahuan snowball is the only *Thelocactus* whose stems are more or less obscured by spines. Its glassy white spines are arranged in a tidy crosshatched pattern that makes it less shaggy-looking than other cactus species with long, white spines. In older plants, offsets can form around the base, but the plants typically seen in cultivation are single-headed.

DESIGN SUGGESTIONS
Exceptional when planted near drought-tolerant perennials with lavender flowers such as *Penstemon amphorellae*

CULTIVATION
Chihuahuan snowball is not fussy, but best in at least moderately well-drained soil, preferably with limestone grit such as dolomitic limestone added to the mix.

This low, broad-growing cactus has sculptural nipples that rise up in high relief like a stylized waffle iron. Combine that with its comely pink flowers and small stature and you have a winning cactus for many garden situations.

Thelocactus rinconensis

bird's nest cactus

NATIVE HABITAT

Coahuila and Nuevo León, Mexico

MATURE SIZE

To 3 inches (7.6 cm) tall and 3–8 inches (7.6–20 cm) across

HARDINESS

Zone 8b

FLOWERING SEASON

Midsummer to early autumn

► The nipples (tubercles) of *Thelocactus rinconensis* are conical, angled, and prominent, giving the plant a very interesting architectural appearance. Its spines (usually 2–4) pop out from the top of the nipples like rabbit ear antennae. Bird's nest cactus grows in limestone slopes and rubble and is often found growing beside annual wildflowers or desert-adapted shrubs. Its flowers are white to light pink and are borne from the center of the stem. The body of the plant is green to blue-green.

DESIGN SUGGESTIONS

Excellent clustered around rockery and boulders. Try planting bird's nest cactus alongside fairy duster (*Calliandra* species) and Texas ranger (*Leucophyllum* species) shrubs and mixing with wildflowers and agaves such as *Agave lophantha*.

CULTIVATION

It is a slow grower, flowering after 5–6 years from seed, but is not bothered by red spider mites, which can attack other species.

NOTABLE VARIETIES, FORMS, AND SUBSPECIES

All but one of the forms of *Thelocactus rinconensis* have been recently disqualified as subspecies. However, these forms, which do vary in their morphology, are still in the trade under their former subspecies names. A nearly, and sometimes completely, spineless form of the bird's nest cactus, *Thelocactus rinconensis* subsp. *phymatothelos* (often sold as *T. phymatothelos*), has lighter pink flowers and more rounded tubercles. *Thelocactus rinconensis* subsp. *freudenbergeri* (pictured) has brighter pink flowers and a lower flattop form with gray-blue flesh.

BIRD'S NEST CACTUS (THE FORM KNOWN IN THE TRADE AS *THELOCACTUS RINCONENSIS* SUBSP. *FREUDENBERGERI*), IN HABITAT NEAR SALTILLO, MEXICO, GROWING BESIDE A FAIRY DUSTER (*CALLIANDRA* SPECIES) SHRUB.

Barrels and Globes

THE BARRELS AND GLOBES are striking for their spherical or cylindrical bodies, which are most often solitary. Perhaps the most recognizable plant in this group is the golden barrel cactus (*Echinocactus grusonii*), whose yellow-gold spines and rounded form make it perhaps the most popular of all garden cactus. Spectacularly colored spines are not limited to the golden barrel—many plants in this group have spines that range from russet to candy-apple red. A good portion of the barrels have blossoms that appear in concentric halo patterns on the crown of the plant. While some are relatively small and spherical in shape, others form fat cylinders and shorter columns.

ASTROPHYTUMS CLUSTERED TOGETHER, AS THEY ARE IN THIS POTTED ARRANGEMENT, COMBINE FOR MAXIMUM IMPACT.

THE INTRICATE FLECKS AND DIVERSITY OF
MARKINGS DISTINGUISH THIS SEED-GROWN
BATCH OF SAND DOLLAR CACTUS.

BISHOP'S CAP CACTUS OFTEN GROW
FASTER WHEN PLANTED IN THE GROUND IN
APPROPRIATE CLIMATES.

▶ Among the most intriguing of all cactus plants, genus *Astrophytum* grows in shapes that have been compared to a bishop's cap, sand dollar, sea urchin, goat's horns, and star. In Greek, the prefix *aster* means star and the suffix *phyton* means plant: therefore the astrophytums are star plants. These star species all come from northern and central Mexico, with one species creeping north into Texas. Compared with the other globe- and barrel-shaped plants listed in this chapter, they are rather low-growing. Astrophytums combine particularly well with trunk-forming yuccas such as *Yucca rostrata* and *Y. faxoniana*, or with green-colored agaves like *Agave parviflora*, *A. ocahui*, or *A. schidigera*.

ECCENTRIC HANDMADE POTS
ACCENTUATE THE EXTRATERRESTRI-
AL FORM OF BISHOP'S CAP CACTUS.

'SUPER KABUTO' OR 'SUPER K' IS ONE OF SEVERAL
EXCITING JAPANESE-BRED *ASTROPHYTUM* CACTUS.

'ONZUKA' IS A JAPANESE-BRED *ASTROPHYTUM*.
THESE WHITE-FLECKED PLANTS LOOK
PARTICULARLY GOOD NEXT TO COLORED WALLS.

Stars of the Garden

Astrophytum asterias

sand dollar cactus; sea urchin cactus

NATIVE HABITAT	MATURE SIZE	HARDINESS	FLOWERING SEASON
South Texas, Nuevo León, and Tamaulipas, Mexico	1–2 inches (2.5–5.1 cm) high and 2.5–7 inches (6.4–18 cm) across	Zone 9	Summer

► Barely popping up above ground, sand dollar cactus is segmented into eight pie-shaped pieces by shallow wrinkles. Sprinkled on top of the flesh is a mirror-image dusting of pure-white flecks, although they are highly variable when grown from seed, and some plants have almost no flocking. Larger polka dot tufts are distributed symmetrically. It is an unusual and fetching plant. It produces yellow flowers with a red center over the summer months. In its native habitat—along the Texas border and south into northeastern Mexico—native populations of the sand dollar cactus have been compromised by overcollection; this may be the result of the plant being mistaken for peyote cactus, or perhaps because the sand dollar cactus is reputed to have mind-altering properties of its own. It has also suffered habitat loss due to agriculture. In any case, it is listed as endangered in the U.S. Endangered Species Act and is afforded the highest level of protection under Appendix I of the CITES treaty. Therefore, gardeners should only purchase plants grown from seed; thankfully such plants are readily available at cactus nurseries.

CULINARY VALUE

Sometimes consumed for its weaker, but supposedly peyote-like effects.

DESIGN SUGGESTIONS

Its sea urchin appearance can be exploited by including sand dollar cactus in an "under-the-sea" themed garden of succulent plants. It is also excellent in a low bowl mixed with other low-growing cactus such as peyote or peyote verde cactus.

CULTIVATION

When grown in full sun, sand dollar cactus's body turns an eerie brown-green, yet in lower light nursery situations, the flesh is often medium or even dark green. In containers, it is sensitive to overwatering in hot, humid weather.

NOTABLE VARIETIES, FORMS, AND SUBSPECIES

A heavily white-flocked cultivar bred in Japan, *Astrophytum asterias* 'Super Kabuto', is strikingly handsome, yet even slower growing that the regular form. Some forms of *A. asterias* 'Super Kabuto' have strongly V-shaped white markings on their bodies. Many other speckled and flocked forms are available in Thailand and Japan.

Strongly resembling both a sand dollar and a sea urchin, this nearly flat, spineless cactus is specked and flecked with white markings and is a must-have curiosity for one's collection.

A PLUMP SAND DOLLAR CACTUS IN ALL OF ITS LOVELY SYMMETRY, GROWING HAPPILY IN CONTAINER CULTURE.

Astrophytum capricorne

goat's horn

Spectacularly upturned brown and black spines coif the crown of goat's horn, making it an indispensable plant for those with an eye for the bizarre.

NATIVE HABITAT	**MATURE SIZE**	**HARDINESS**	**FLOWERING SEASON**
Coahuila, Mexico, and elsewhere in the Chihuahuan Desert	4–10 inches (10–25 cm) high and 4–6 inches (10–15 cm) wide	Zone 8b	Early to late summer

► Underneath the upturned and twisting spines of goat's horn is a handsome body. The body can be lightly or heavily flocked with white spots and resembles a wild-haired version of its close cousin *Astrophytum ornatum*. When goat's horn flowers, its buds rise up through the wavy spines and open chiffon yellow with a carmine red center. Another of goat horn's assets is its sweetly fragrant bloom.

CULINARY VALUE

Reported use—as with most plants in this genus—as an inferior peyote substitute

DESIGN SUGGESTIONS

Goat's horn is excellent grouped together in a low bowl mingling with other members of genus *Astrophytum*.

CULTIVATION

This cactus is not tolerant of overwatering and overpotting—don't be afraid to cram it in a smallish pot.

NOTABLE VARIETIES, FORMS, AND SUBSPECIES

Astrophytum capricorne forma *senile* has very heavy and crazy spination and light flocking. The interlacing frazzle of spines on its crown is much heavier than on the regular goat's horn. It is often sold as *Astrophytum senile*.

A POTTED GOAT'S HORN AT TUCSON BOTANICAL GARDENS.

Astrophytum myriostigma

bishop's cap;
bishop's miter cactus

Bishop's cap has a clean architectural look, no spines, and an even covering of white scales giving its skin an almost felt-like appearance. Its spineless nature and unusual form make bishop's cap a must-have for beginners or aficionados.

NATIVE HABITAT

Northern and central Mexico, primarily in the Chihuahuan Desert

MATURE SIZE

4–12 inches (10–30 cm) high and 4–7 inches (10–18 cm) across

HARDINESS

Zone 8b

FLOWERING SEASON

Late spring to late summer

▶ The evenly distributed white dots that cover the bishop's cap look as though they were put there by the tip of a pointillist painter's brush or perhaps created digitally, but this polka-dot flocking is more than just aesthetic. It actually reflects light and thus protects the plant from sunburn. The form of the plant undeniably resembles its namesake clerical headwear. Bishop's cap typically has five segmented ribs and produces glossy yellow flowers from the center of the top of its stem.

DESIGN SUGGESTIONS

A superb plant to cluster in a pot, or for use in a sensory garden (thanks to their lack of spines) where they can be touched.

CULTIVATION

Bishop's cap is generally quite easy to grow, but because it comes from the summer rainfall regime of the Chihuahuan Desert, winter watering is best avoided. Like monk's hood cactus, *Astrophytum myriostigma* seems to plump up and thrive when grown in the ground in appropriate climates. Rabbits will sometimes browse bishop's cap.

NOTABLE VARIETIES, FORMS, AND SUBSPECIES

An unusual form of bishop's cap, *Astrophytum myriostigma* var. *nudum*, is as its name suggests, rather naked. The vestment it lacks is the

white flocking and thus its skin has only a light green waxy appearance. Because of this lack of white scales, it is less tolerant of full sun and reflected heat than the straight species. Another exceptional plant is *A. myriostigma* 'Onzuka'. This Japanese form typically has four ribs, numerous white markings, and often chevron-shaped markings along each rib.

NESTLED AMONG ROCKS, THIS FAT AND HAPPY BISHOP'S CAP IS PLANTED IN THE GROUND IN THE DEMONSTRATION GARDEN AT STARR NURSERY IN TUCSON, ARIZONA.

A MONK'S HOOD CACTUS PLANTED IN THE GROUND.

Astrophytum ornatum

monk's hood; star cactus

NATIVE HABITAT	MATURE SIZE	HARDINESS	FLOWERING SEASON
Hidalgo and Querétaro, Mexico	12–39 inches (30–100 cm) high and 6–12 inches (15–30 cm) wide	Zone 8b	Summer

▶ The tallest plant in genus *Astrophytum*, old specimens of monk's hood cactus can grow up to waist high. Their deep green bodies are lightly flecked with interesting pixilated-looking white markings. The body of monk's hood cactus is segmented by five to eight ribs that sometimes twist into a spiral growth pattern. The yellow to brown spines contrast nicely with its green body. Shiny yellow flowers emerge from the center of the plant, followed by fruit that forms a star pattern when viewed from above.

DESIGN SUGGESTIONS

Handsome when in the ground and massed in a group of three or five plants adjacent to boulders. Also very effective similarly clustered in a low bowl.

CULTIVATION

If your climate is warm enough, plant monk's hood cactus in the ground, where it tends to grow larger and more robust in a shorter time period. Avoid winter watering.

NOTABLE VARIETIES, FORMS, AND SUBSPECIES

One of the most stunning plants in all of genus *Astrophytum* is *A. ornatum* var. *mirbellii*. It is heavily flocked with white that makes its yellow-orange spines jump into high relief. It is a gem that stands out in any collection of cactus.

Monk's hood is the largest, fastest, and easiest to grow of all plants in genus *Astrophytum*. It forms a single green cylinder freckled with intricate white dots and handsome spines.

ASTROPHYTUM ORNATUM VAR. *MIRBELLII* SHOWS OFF ITS WHITE FLOCKING.

NO OTHER CACTUS PLANTINGS ARE AS ICONIC AND RECOGNIZABLE AS MASS PLANTED
GOLDEN BARRELS—SHOWCASED HERE AT THE DESERT BOTANICAL GARDEN IN PHOENIX.

A NICHOL'S TURK'S HEAD CACTUS
SHOWING A FLASH OF PINK BLOOM FOL-
LOWING SUMMER RAINS.

▷ Sometimes confused with barrel cactus in the genus *Ferocactus*, *Echinocactus* differs in that all have woolly stem tips as they mature. Over the years as botanists moved cactus plants from one classification to another, as many as 1000 species were at one time called *Echinocactus*—now only six species remain. Thankfully the remaining six are remarkable garden plants. I share five of the six species here.

TWIN TURK'S HEAD CACTUS ARE THE FOCUS OF
THIS PROMINENT CONTAINER PLANTING.

AN IMPRESSIVE MANY-HEADED BARREL
SPECIMEN THRIVING ON THE LAVA FIELDS OF
MEXICO'S PINACATE WILDERNESS.

DESERT WILDFLOWERS AND PERENNIALS SUCH AS DESERT BLUEBELLS
AND DAMIANITA DAISY KNIT TOGETHER THE SPACES BETWEEN
GOLDEN BARREL CACTUS AT THE DESERT BOTANICAL GARDEN IN PHOENIX.

Hail to the Woolly Topped Barrels

A CLASSIC IN-GROUND MASS PLANTING OF MATURE GOLDEN BARREL CACTUS.

Likely the most popularly grown and sought-after landscape cactus in the world, golden barrel cactus's fat spherical shape and veritably glowing yellow spines are its siren song.

Echinocactus grusonii

golden barrel cactus

NATIVE HABITAT	MATURE SIZE	HARDINESS	FLOWERING SEASON
Guanajuato, Hildalgo, Querértaro, and San Luis Potosí, Mexico	8 inches to 4.25 feet high (20 cm–1.3 m) high and 16–31 inches (40–78.5 cm) across	Zone 8b	Summer, fall, spring

► Golden barrel is a plant you grow for the spines—which when grown in full sun are a rich glowing gold that almost defies description. Although they usually grow singly, clustered plants with two to five heads can be found in the nursery trade. In their native habitat in Mexico, the plants have nearly disappeared due to overharvesting, and dam and road construction. Thankfully, the supply of nursery plants is more than ample and in the Southwest and Southern California, they are grown in tens of thousands, perhaps even hundreds of thousands. The current oversupply is in part due to Chinese demand. During the 1990s, owning a large and vibrant golden barrel cactus was thought to imbue prosperity to its Chinese owners; as a result, entire shipping containers of barrel cactus were sent from California nurseries to Chinese ports. Sadly, the fad didn't last and the result has been a glut of the plants in the market; the upside of this surfeit of golden barrels is that large landscape-sized specimens are now available at bargain prices. In the right climate, the golden barrel can achieve truly massive proportions and will grow to over 4 feet (1.2 m) high! Its flowers are a gold color similar to the spines and are therefore not particularly showy, although the monochromatic gold crown they add to the plant is handsome. Older plants grow a scull cap-sized patch of cream-colored wool on the tops of their stems.

DESIGN SUGGESTIONS

Planting great masses of golden barrel cactus in courtyards has become so common that is it almost a cliché. However, grouping them is still visually effective, especially when they are paired with silver-leafed succulents such as *Yucca rostrata*.

CULTIVATION

The spines grow more dense and darker gold when grown in full sun. Also, the plants will not flower until they are at least 14 inches (35 cm) across. They must be grown in full sun for best gold coloration.

Easily identified by its stout claw-like stems, blue-green flesh, and large pink flowers. One of the best single-headed barrel type species for garden cultivation.

Echinocactus horizonthalonius

Turk's head cactus; devil's head cactus; eagle's claw

NATIVE HABITAT

Widespread throughout the Chihuahuan Desert region, including southwest Texas, New Mexico, and Mexico

MATURE SIZE

To 12 inches (30 cm) high and 4–6 inches (10–15 cm) across

HARDINESS

Zone 7

FLOWERING SEASON

Early spring to midsummer, depending on elevation and rainfall

▶ All of the spines on the Turk's head cactus are big and beefy and grow along the ridges of its eight ribs. It is almost always a solitary plant, although small clumps with two or occasionally three heads are sometimes found. It is one of the smallest *Echinocactus* and the only plant in the genus that will bloom reliably in a pot. The thick spines interlace, stretching nearly from rib to rib, but not quite obscuring the attractive gray-green to blue-green flesh. The flowers are large pink affairs—up to 3 inches (7.6 cm) across—and contrast nicely with the body and spines. The plants flower following heavy summer rains and most plants in a geographic area will bloom on the same day. It can bloom up to six times per year, although each bloom typically lasts only one to three days.

CULINARY VALUE

In the past, the flesh of this plant was used to make cactus candy, which, given its value as an ornamental plant, seems shamelessly wasteful today.

DESIGN SUGGESTIONS

Spectacular massed in a scree-filled gravel garden or near the front of a border where their handsome heads can be seen up close. Equally impressive in container culture.

CULTIVATION

Turk's head cactus needs bright sun for best growth and flowering; it will also gladly tolerate reflected heat. It typically grows in limestone rubble, so adding dolomitic limestone to your soil mix is a good idea.

NOTABLE VARIETIES, FORMS, AND SUBSPECIES

A rare relic population from an earlier time, *Echinocactus horizonthalonius* subsp. *nicholii* (Nichol Turk's head) is restricted to just a few limestone mountain ranges in Sonora and central Arizona. It is similar to regular Turk's head, but grows taller, up to 20 inches (51 cm). Listed as threatened with extinction under the U.S. Endangered Species Act, it has been poached to such an extent that individual plants in Arizona are marked with metal numbered tags and monitored for theft.

**FLOWERING
TURK'S HEAD IN
HABITAT IN THE
CHIHUAHUAN
DESERT.**

Echinocactus platyacanthus
(Also sold as *Echinocactus ingens*)

giant barrel cactus; large barrel cactus

Far and away the largest of all barrel cactus, giant barrel is notable for its oval woody cap, bright gold flowers, and bright green flesh.

NATIVE HABITAT

Central Mexico—Southern Coahuila to Puebla

MATURE SIZE

2–8.5 feet (0.6–2.5 m) tall and 16–31 inches (40–78.5 cm) across

HARDINESS

Zone 9b

FLOWERING SEASON

Mid- to late summer

A MATURE GIANT BARREL IN HABITAT IN THE MEXICAN STATE OF SAN LUIS POTOSÍ.

► The undisputed size champion for barrel cactus, giant barrel's mature height and width can reach 8 feet (2.4 m) high and almost 3 feet (91 cm) wide! Its juvenile form looks very different than its adult appearance. In youth, it has gray-green flesh and purple chevron patterns around the crown; the spines are reddish purple. As an adult, a broad oval of cream-colored wool forms on top of the stem, the flesh takes on much brighter green tones, and the spines become blackish. Even side by side, it is difficult for the uninitiated to recognize that a juvenile and adult giant barrel are the same species of cactus. On very old specimens the wool cap is so large that the center of the plant appears thornless. The bright yellow-gold flowers emerge directly from the wool.

DESIGN SUGGESTIONS

Dramatic when planted in the ground flanking an entryway. Equally impressive planted in masses in a courtyard. Giant barrels pair exceptionally well with large trunk-forming yuccas such as *Yucca faxoniana*.

CULTIVATION

Full sun and good drainage. Make sure to protect from cold damp soil in winter.

Echinocactus polycephalus

many-headed barrel; cottontop cactus

This long-lived and exceptionally slow grower is armed with a web of stiff interlocking spines; it produces dozens of individual heads that eventually form a hemisphere of stems.

NATIVE HABITAT	**MATURE SIZE**	**HARDINESS**	**FLOWERING SEASON**
Western and northwestern Arizona, southeastern California, southern Nevada, southwestern Utah, and northwestern Sonora, Mexico	12–24 inches (30–60 cm) high and 2–3.5 feet (30–100 cm) across	Zone 7b	Late spring to early summer

▶ The many-headed barrel can have up to 100 stems (heads), 6 to 8 inches wide (15–20 cm). Although their spines are red, they often appear white or light pink thanks to a white felt that covers the spines; following rain, the usually dull spines turn a brilliant red. *Echinocactus polycephalus* grows on inhospitable, dry, rocky slopes and volcanic plains and outcrops in areas where temperatures can shoot past 115° F (46° C), making it one of the most heat-tolerant species conceivable. The flowers of the many-headed barrel are yellow and are so imbedded within the mesh of spines that they are unable to fully open. They are, however, highly perfumed—if one can get his or her nose close to them! The flower buds are covered with dense wool-like hairs, reflected in its other common name, cottontop cactus.

DESIGN SUGGESTIONS

Plant many-headed barrel singly in a large, low bowl, or if planted in the ground, pair it with desert sage (*Salvia dorrii*).

CULTIVATION

Full-blasting sun, fast drainage, and patience are most of what is needed.

NOTABLE VARIETIES, FORMS, AND SUBSPECIES

Echinocactus polycephalus subsp. *xeranthemoides* is generally a smaller plant, seldom producing more than 12 stems. It grows at higher elevations (3300–4900 feet, 1000–1500 m) in pinyon-juniper woodlands. It is found perched on the rim of the Grand Canyon.

A LARGE MANY-HEADED BARREL CACTUS IN HABITAT IN MEXICO'S PINACATE WILDERNESS.

A FLOWERING HORSE CRIPPLER PLANTED IN THE GROUND IN AN EL PASO, TEXAS, GARDEN.

A low-growing mounding hemisphere, the horse crippler is one of the most common cactus on the lower Great Plains. It is also one of the easiest to grow and rewards gardeners with salmon-pink flowers in late spring.

Echinocactus texensis

horse crippler

NATIVE HABITAT

The western two-thirds of Texas, southeastern New Mexico, southwestern Oklahoma, and also in Coahuila, Nuevo León, and Tamaulipas, Mexico

MATURE SIZE

6–8 inches (15–20 cm) tall and 6–12 inches (15–30 cm) across

HARDINESS

Zone 7

FLOWERING SEASON

Mid- to late spring

▶ As its name suggests, the horse crippler is not equine-friendly, but it is a boon to gardeners. It keeps a low (usually less than 6 inches high) profile and grows in saline flats, thornscrub, grasslands, and oak woodlands. Sturdy spines line its 13 ribs and can puncture the tender flesh beneath a horse's hoof. The stem is rock hard and isn't harmed when accidentally stepped upon (don't attempt this without heavy-soled boots). In a garden, it is known for its low care and pink to salmon-pink flowers. The flowers often sport hot-pink throats that contrast nicely with the lighter pink petals. The horse crippler tolerates cold, humid conditions better than most other cactus species. It is known to overwinter well even in cool, damp Victoria, British Columbia.

CULINARY VALUE

Its body was used to make cactus candy in the past.

DESIGN SUGGESTIONS

Horse crippler is an excellent choice potted with wildflowers such as lupine or Mexican gold poppy.

CULTIVATION

No special instructions

THE COLORFUL AND LONG-PERSISTING YELLOW FRUIT OF THE FISHHOOK BARREL ARE COMPLEMENTED BY TRUE-BLUE WILDFLOWERS LIKE THESE DESERT BLUEBELLS.

THE COMPASS BARREL IN BLOOM SPORTS A RING OF CONCENTRIC FLOWERS AROUND ITS CROWN.

▶ The barrel cactus get their botanical genus name, *Ferocactus*, from the Latin prefix *ferox*, meaning wild, fierce, or ferocious. While it is true that many in this group have long-hooked spines, they are well behaved in a garden setting. Especially in the warmer parts of the southwestern United States, they are key elements in xeric landscapes. They all grow into either squat or more upright barrel shapes, flower during the day, and are pollinated by bees. Most bear flowers in rings around their tops, but they are more sought after for their spines than their flowers; members of this genus have gold, red, pink, or gray spines. One showstopper species has spines that jet straight out of the plant up to 10 inches (25 cm) in length. In pots, most species will do well provided they are put out in full sunlight during the warm months and are up-potted frequently to accommodate their increasing girth.

A FAMILY OF THE UNBELIEVABLY LONG-SPINED BAJA PUNK ROCK BARREL CACTUS FORM
A FOCAL POINT IN A GARDEN AT THE ARIZONA-SONORA DESERT MUSEUM.

A MATURE FISHHOOK BARREL SPORTS A HALO
OF ORANGE/RED FLOWERS IN SEASON.

Fear Not the Ferocious Barrels

Ferocactus chrysacanthus

Baja yellow barrel

Its dense web of yellow to yellow-orange spines makes the Baja yellow barrel a much sought-after barrel cactus for collectors seeking a yellow-spined alternative to the ubiquitous golden barrel cactus.

NATIVE HABITAT

Isla Cedros and San Benito off the Pacific coast of Baja California, Mexico

MATURE SIZE

3.25 feet (1 m) tall and 12 inches (30 cm) across

HARDINESS

Zone 9

FLOWERING SEASON

Early summer; early autumn to midautumn in temperate climates

► Endemic to two islands off the Pacific coast of Baja, the Baja yellow barrel is a rare plant in nature that has become fairly common in cactus nurseries. One look at the colorful, dense spines and you are hooked. They range from a vibrant yellow-gold to a more subdued but equally handsome orange-brown or occasional red. By most accounts it's a frustratingly slow-growing plant, taking around 10 years to reach its flowering size (yellow-orange blooms), about 6 inches (15 cm) in diameter. It is not the flowers that make the plant such an interesting addition to a garden, however, but rather its fabulous spines.

DESIGN SUGGESTIONS

Baja yellow barrels are wonderful when planted in vivid-colored glazed pottery, particularly deep reds and cobalt blues.

CULTIVATION

Patience is the key virtue needed to grow this cactus; plants that have a diameter smaller than 3 to 4 inches (7.6–10 cm) are neither hard to find in nurseries, nor terribly expensive.

A POTTED BAJA YELLOW BARREL IN A TUCSON, ARIZONA, GARDEN.

Ferocactus cylindraceus
(Also sold as *Ferocactus acanthodes*)

compass barrel; California barrel

The compass barrel cactus gets its common name from its tendency to lean toward the southwest.

NATIVE HABITAT

Much of central and southern Arizona, southwestern Utah in the Mojave Desert, inland Southern California, Baja California, and Sonora, Mexico

MATURE SIZE

1.5–7 feet (0.45–2.1 m) tall and up to 24 inches (60 cm) in diameter

HARDINESS

Zone 7b

FLOWERING SEASON

Early spring to early summer

▶ Compass barrels are topped with a dense mesh of spines. They bear yellow flowers that open before many other cactus species. The spines vary in color from red to russet to yellow and resemble stiff, coarse hair combed up toward the tip of the plant. After a rain, the spines appear lacquered and glow. The compass barrel is exceedingly tough and grows in drier situations than other members of genus *Ferocactus*. In fact, researchers have proved that after acclimation, compass barrels can withstand temperatures of up to an astounding 154° F (68° C)! Given a favorably warm spot, compass barrel can eventually get as tall as a man; hence, the Seri Indian name for the compass barrel which translates to "thinks it's a saguaro." Sometime in either the 19th or early 20th century, a myth began that the barrel cactus contained a reservoir of water suitable for quenching the thirst of desert travelers. Although the flesh of the plant does hold water, extracting an amount suitable for drinking is extremely difficult. The barrel cactus was also turned into cactus candy in Southern California, nearly wiping out wild populations east of Los Angeles. Sometimes compass barrels grow directly out of fissures in canyon walls.

DESIGN SUGGESTIONS

Superb for rock gardens. Try combining compass barrel with desert agave (*Agave deserti*) and penstemon species that grow in rocky habitat. It is also handsome combined with rock-colonizing hedgehog species.

CULTIVATION

Plant in fast-draining soil. In containers, use a cactus and succulent potting soil (sold as cactus mix). In the ground, avoid situations where the plant could sit in water by planting on mounds. Use long tweezers to remove weeds growing in the spine mesh.

A BLOOMING COMPASS BARREL IN HABITAT IN BAJA CALIFORNIA NORTE, MEXICO.

Ferocactus emoryi
(Also sold as *Ferocactus covillei*)

Coville barrel

Coville barrel is grown for its tidy appearance
and arresting red flower rings.

NATIVE HABITAT

Central and western Arizona, as well as western
Sonora, Mexico

MATURE SIZE

2–8 feet (0.6–2.4 cm)
tall and up to 39 inches
(1 m) across

HARDINESS

Zone 8b

**FLOWERING
SEASON**

Late summer to
early autumn

► Although similar to its relative, the fishhook
barrel, Coville barrel has two major distinguish-
ing characteristics. Its body is more gray-green
and it lacks hairlike radial spines. For landscape
use, its lack of these thin radial spines imparts
a cleaner, less-shaggy appearance. It is almost
always a single stemmed cylinder. Most of the
plants in the trade bear deep red flowers in rings
around the tip of the stem. Following flowering,
small pineapple-shaped fruit persist on the plant
for many months and turn yellow as they ripen,
adding winter interest and color. When young,
Coville barrel has prominent tubercles and a
gray or blue-gray cast to its skin.

DESIGN SUGGESTIONS

Nice mixed with yellow- and orange-flowered
fishhook barrel cactus, or planted on its own in
a sizable vessel

CULTIVATION

It may take as long as 15–20 years to flower if
grown from seed, but larger seed-grown plants
are often available from nurseries for those without the time and/or patience.

A MATURE COVILLE
BARREL STANDS
TALL AT THE DES-
ERT BOTANICAL
GARDEN, PHOE-
NIX, ARIZONA.

Ferocactus emoryi subsp. *rectispinus*
(Also sold as *Ferocactus rectispinus*)

Baja punk rock barrel; hatpin barrel

Far and away the longest-spined of all barrel cactus, the shockingly erect spines of Baja punk rock barrel make it a brassy and bold addition to a garden.

NATIVE HABITAT	MATURE SIZE	HARDINESS	FLOWERING SEASON
Northern Baja California Sur	Up to 5 feet (1.5 m) high with a diameter of 18 inches (45 cm)	Zone 9	Midummer to early autumn

▶ The spines of the Baja punk rock barrel, unlike most members of the genus, exhibit almost no hooking. They are as straight and gravity defying as a super-glued Mohawk hairdo. Because the spine length is variable—ranging from long to "whoa daddy"—enthusiasts try to outdo each other by finding a specimen with the longest central spines. Some specimens have central spines that exceed 10 inches (25 cm) in length. Similarly, the spine color also varies from white to a sought-after deep pinkish red, so it is best to inspect the plants in person when making a selection. Until recently *Ferocactus emoryi* subsp. *rectispinus* was its own species but has now been brought back under *emoryi*. Baja punk rock barrel attains considerably smaller mature stature than regular *F. emoryi*, which in some ways makes it more desirable as a landscape plant. It is nearly always solitary. Its flowers range from yellow to medium gold and are generated in the center of the plant. After flowering, attractive, straw-topped fruit persists on the plant for many months.

DESIGN SUGGESTIONS

This cactus is equally arresting solo in a broad, low bowl or planted in the ground *en masse*. In a pot, sow desert bluebells (*Phacelia campanularia*) seed in the gravel around the Baja punk rock barrel.

CULTIVATION

More frost sensitive then Coville barrel, Baja punk rock barrel needs protection from hard freezes.

A LARGE, POTTED BAJA PUNK ROCK BARREL AT THE ARIZONA-SONORA DESERT MUSEUM.

One of the only barrel cactus with a true blue blush to its skin, the blue barrel is nicely accented with yellow spines and flowers.

Ferocactus glaucescens

blue barrel

NATIVE HABITAT

Hildalgo, Querétaro, and San Luis Potosí

MATURE SIZE

18 inches (45 cm) and 20 inches (51 cm) across

HARDINESS

Zone 9

FLOWERING SEASON

Early summer to midsummer

► As yellow-spined barrel cactus go, perhaps the blue barrel is a bit understated in comparison with its flashier cousin, the golden barrel cactus. Nonetheless, the blue barrel is a garden plant with its own charms, namely its blue-green stems. In fact, those with golden barrel fatigue should consider the blue barrel as a sophisticated alternative. Blue barrel's broad blue stems are accented with butter-yellow spines along its ridges. Usually solitary or occasionally multi-stemmed, it is often wider than it is tall. *Ferocactus glaucescens* is less densely spined than many of the barrels, making its handsome blue skin more visible. Its flowers, which are also a light yellow, seem to be just the right color value to contrast with the blue stems.

DESIGN SUGGESTIONS

Very effective when planted alongside bishop's cap cactus or other *Astrophytum* species

CULTIVATION

A relatively fast-growing cactus in cultivation, plants will begin blooming after a few years and continue reliably every year thereafter. It is sometimes susceptible to sooty mold in greenhouses, which can blemish its blue skin.

AN IN-GROUND
PLANTING OF
BLUE BARREL
CACTUS AT
STARR NURSERY
IN TUCSON,
ARIZONA.

A YOUNG BAJA FIRE BARREL GROWING IN HABITAT OUT OF A GRANITE BOULDER IN BAJA CALIFORNIA NORTE, MEXICO.

Characterized by wide, red spines that turn a vibrant crimson after a rainstorm, it may be the most desirable of all the red-spined barrel cactus.

Ferocactus gracilis subsp. *coloratus*
(Also sold as *Ferocactus gracilis* var. *coloratus*; *Ferocactus coloratus*)

Baja fire barrel

NATIVE HABITAT	MATURE SIZE	HARDINESS	FLOWERING SEASON
Central Baja California near Cataviña	Usually less than 39 inches (100 cm) tall and around 12 inches (30 cm) across	Zone 9	Early summer to midsummer

► Its broad, concave spines range from medium pink to candy-apple red. The spines on the best specimens are densely interlaced, forming a netting of red that almost completely obscures the body of the plant. Visually, the effect is that of a barrel with a red body. Completing this rosy picture, the Baja fire barrel produces concentric rings of—you guessed it—red flowers in the summer months. It is distinguished from regular *Ferocactus gracilis* by its stouter, flatter, and broader central spines, as well as its shorter stature.

DESIGN SUGGESTIONS

Baja fire barrel is stunning when clustered or planted in groups, especially when planted adjacent to gold-flowered or silver-leafed, drought-tolerant perennials.

CULTIVATION

A fickle flowerer in cultivation, some plants may take 20 years to produce flowers, or may never produce flowers at all. In the hot parts of the Southwest, it is a reliable flowerer when planted in-ground, in full-sun settings.

Ferocactus herrerae
(Also sold as *Ferocactus wizlizeni* subsp. *herrerae*; *Ferocactus horridus*)

twisted barrel cactus

Beefy, grayish white spines give the twisted barrel a well-armed, full metal jacket look that is highly architectural and attractive.

NATIVE HABITAT	**MATURE SIZE**	**HARDINESS**	**FLOWERING SEASON**
The mountains and coastal plains adjacent to the Gulf of California, in the Mexican states of Sinaloa and Sonora	To 6.5 feet (2 m) tall and 18 inches (45 cm) across	Zone 9	Midspring to late summer

WISTED BARREL LOADED WITH FRUIT IN A TUCSON GARDEN DESIGNED BY THE AUTHOR.

► Twisted barrel's prominent broad central spines are handsome and contrast well with its wide, green stem. As it matures, its ribs often grow in a spiral twist, giving rise to its common name. The spines are a grayish white or sometimes brownish, but they sport a satin sheen that makes them look silvery in some light conditions. Around the silvery central and radial spines, some thin, wiry spines also lend interest. The flowers are yellow to yellow-gold (occasionally orange or red) and have red to red-brown midveins. A unique aspect of twisted barrel is how the yellow pineapple-shaped fruit persists not just at the crown of the plant, but well down the ribs, in a fashion much different than other species in the genus. In habitat it can grow as tall as a basketball forward—over 6 feet, 6 inches—although in cultivation is it typically much smaller.

The jury is still out as to whether *F. herrerae* is a separate species (as Anderson lists it, 2001) or a subspecies of *Ferocactus wizlizeni* (Pilbeam and Bowdery). For the sake of gardeners, I've chosen to list it under its most common Latin label in cultivation (*Ferocactus herrerae*) until the matter is more satisfactorily settled.

CULINARY VALUE
The fruit is edible and the seeds are ground into flour by the Seri Indians.

DESIGN SUGGESTIONS
Plant twisted barrel cactus adjacent to wildflowers such as sundrops (*Calylophus hartwegii*), native fleabane (*Erigeron divergens*), and Mexican evening primrose (*Oenothera speciosa*).

CULTIVATION SUGGESTIONS
Although it comes from a mostly frost-free habitat, twisted barrel will withstand below-freezing temperatures for short periods.

Ferocactus latispinus

devil's tongue; crow's claw; candy cactus

With the flattest and most tongue-like spines of any of the barrel cactus, devil's tongue is an excellent species for the garden, with its rakish spines and unusual autumn flowering time.

NATIVE HABITAT	MATURE SIZE	HARDINESS	FLOWERING SEASON
Widely distributed in central Mexico	12 inches (30 cm) tall and 16 inches (40 cm) across	Zone 9b	Midautumn to early winter, mostly in late autumn

▶ Devil's tongue is a squat, solitary hemisphere whose body sports sharply furrowed canyons and angular ribs. Its central spines are very broad and relatively short when compared with most in the genus. The central spines are banded red and gold, and curve downward at the tip like a tongue. Devil's tongue blooms later than almost any of the barrel cactus and its flowers are an unusual, rich purple-pink color (although they are occasionally yellow or cream).

CULINARY VALUE
In the past, the body of the plant was chopped up and pickled in sugar to make candy.

DESIGN SUGGESTIONS
Because of its diminutive size, Devil's tongue is excellent potted, but also nice in a group or collection of barrel cactus planted in the ground where the climate allows.

CULTIVATION
For the best spine development, it needs full, bright light. Because of this cactus's late bloom, northern-climate gardeners with greenhouses should increase inside temperatures to at least 59° F (15° C) to coax blooming. Otherwise, as temperatures cool, they can be brought indoors and placed in a sunny window.

NOTABLE VARIETIES, FORMS, AND SUBSPECIES
In cultivation, you can find white- and yellow-spined forms. Look for plants labeled *Ferocactus latispinus* 'Yellow Spined'.

JUST COMING INTO BLOOM, THIS DEVIL'S TONGUE IN A TUCSON, ARIZONA, LANDSCAPE IS LOADED WITH MORE THAN A DOZEN BUDS THAT WILL BLOOM THROUGHOUT LATE AUTUMN.

SWEET BARREL
FLOWERING AT
B & B CACTUS
FARM IN TUCSON,
ARIZONA.

The spines of the exceptionally low-growing and early-flowering sweet barrel hug the plant in a close embrace, and the pink candy-striped flowers make it a sweet (*dulce*) barrel indeed.

Ferocactus macrodiscus

sweet barrel;
biznaga de dulce

NATIVE HABITAT

Central Mexican highlands—Guanajuato, Oaxaca, Puebla, Querétaro, and San Luis Potosí

MATURE SIZE

4 inches (10 cm) high and 12–16 inches (30–40 cm) across

HARDINESS

Zone 9b

FLOWERING SEASON

Early spring to early summer

► Similar in stature to the horse crippler cactus, the sweet barrel is hard to find in habitat as it hunkers down among grasses and shrubs. However, when it blooms, its candy-striped pink flowers betray its cover. For growers and collectors in cold climates where greenhouse space is at a premium, the small size of sweet barrel makes it desirable. Additionally, it begins blooming when it is only 4 inches (10 cm) in diameter. Its spines are a handsome yellow-white or sometimes puce pink that stand out nicely against the sweet barrel's blue-gray body.

CULINARY VALUE

As with many barrels, its flesh was once used to make cactus candy.

DESIGN SUGGESTIONS

A great plant to show off in a low bowl. Try planting it with the wildflower baby blue eyes (*Nemophilia menziesii*) for a pink and blue effect.

CULTIVATION

Because sweet barrel grows in a summer rainfall area, it can be prone to rot if kept too wet in the winter. Refrain from watering once cold temperatures arrive.

Along with its relative the Baja fire barrel (*Ferocactus gracilis* subsp. *coloratus*), the Mexican fire barrel cactus is without a doubt one of the two most spectacular red-spined plants in the genus.

Ferocactus pilosus
(Also sold as *Ferocactus pringlei*,
Ferocactus stainesii var. *pilosus*)

Mexican fire barrel;
Mexican lime cactus

NATIVE HABITAT	MATURE SIZE	HARDINESS	FLOWERING SEASON
North-central Mexico	As high as 10 feet (3 m) with individual stems to 20 inches (51 cm) in diameter; much smaller in cultivation.	Zone 8b	Late winter to midspring

► In habitat, Mexican fire barrel is quite massive. It can grow singly or in clusters, but in its range, it is not unusual to run across giant 9-foot-diameter clumps shooting up out of the Tamaulipan thornscrub to heights over 9 feet (2.7 m)! The spine color is variable and thus it is best to see before buying. The spines can range from merely dull pink to a deep burgundy red. Additionally, some individual plants take on an attractive red mottling on their bodies along their ribs during the cold months. A few growers have found Mexican fire barrels with red spines and red winter flesh and those plants are truly to die for. Some horticulturists remark that this species is grown for its spines rather than its flowers, but the cup-shaped flaming orange flowers are fetching set against the red spination.

CULINARY VALUE

Its ripe fruit have a juicy pulp that tastes like a lime, leading to one of its common names, Mexican lime cactus.

DESIGN SUGGESTIONS

Planting a series of Mexican fire barrels in pots along a wall or brightly lit windowsill is nearly always attractive. Mexican fire barrels make a great substitute for the more common golden barrel cactus in mass plantings.

CULTIVATION

Keep in mind that in greenhouse conditions, Mexican fire barrel is not a reliable bloomer; it needs strong light and heat in the summer months to flower.

NOTABLE VARIETIES, FORMS, AND SUBSPECIES

A form of the plant, which is sometimes sold as *Ferocactus stainsii*, has numerous white, radial, thread-like spines.

MEXICAN FIRE
BARREL IN HABITAT
NEAR REAL DE
CATORCE IN SAN
LUIS POTOSÍ,
MEXICO.

A LARGE CLUMP BARREL NEARLY BUSTING OUT OF ITS POT IN MILES ANDERSON'S PERSONAL COLLECTION.

Unlike any of the other barrel cactus, the clump barrel grows into a massive spreading colony comprised of hundreds of arms. It looks more like a hedgehog than the usually singular barrel species.

Ferocactus robustus

clump barrel

NATIVE HABITAT	MATURE SIZE	HARDINESS	FLOWERING SEASON
Puebla, Mexico	Up to 3.3 feet (1 m) tall and 16 feet across (4.8 m), much smaller in cultivation	Zone 9	Mid- to late summer

► In the thin limestone flats of Puebla, Mexico, the clump barrel can achieve truly giant proportions—growing to over 15 feet (nearly 4.5 m) across and up to 3 feet (nearly 1 m) high. The stems are a nice bright green color and have short brown to reddish spines. Each individual head is only about 4 inches (10 cm) across. Clump barrel does have nice yellow blooms, but in a garden situation, this is a plant to grow for its form as it is known to be a recalcitrant flowerer in cultivation.

DESIGN SUGGESTIONS

A broad, low pot is the best display vessel for the clump barrel.

CULTIVATION

Ferocactus robustus tends to develop brown marks around the base of its stems, particularly in older plants. Frequent up-potting is recommended, as is keeping it warm and dry over the winter months.

A big spherical plant with hooked spines. At maturity, it serves as a flower-crowned sculpture in a garden.

Ferocactus wislizeni

fishhook barrel; candy barrel; Arizona barrel

NATIVE HABITAT

South-central Arizona; southwestern New Mexico; around El Paso, Texas; northeastern Sonora and north-western Chihuahua, Mexico

MATURE SIZE

3–5 feet high (0.9–1.5 m) and 2 feet (60 cm) wide. Exceptional specimens can be up to 10 feet (3 m) high.

HARDINESS

Zone 8

FLOWERING SEASON

Midsummer to midautumn

► The Seri Indians used *Ferocactus wislizeni* spines as fishhooks and its flowers for face paint. In a garden, it is equally useful. Midsummer to midautumn, rings of yellow, orange, or red blooms appear on the top of its stems. It has year-round interest: rings of yellow, pineapple-shaped fruit persist over the cool months. Like its cousin the compass barrel, fishhook barrel often tilts toward the southwest. Extremely long-lived—to over 130 years old—*F. wislizeni* can weigh several hundred pounds at maturity. Several cactus and succulent societies salvage and sell fishhook barrels that are growing on land slated for development.

CULINARY VALUE

The yellow, pineapple-shaped fruit can be sliced, seeded, and served like a slightly sour, crunchy cucumber.

DESIGN SUGGESTIONS

An excellent species for pots, or where applicable, clustered *en masse*. Fishhook barrel looks smart paired with wildflowers such as desert marigold (*Baileya multiradiata*) and desert bluebells (*Phacelia campanularia*).

CULTIVATION

A forgiving plant; when transplanting, the fishhook barrel can sit for months, perhaps years, before replanting. Move fishhook barrels with pieces of old carpet and use heavy leather welder's gloves to handle them.

NOTABLE VARIETIES, FORMS, AND SUBSPECIES

A handsome and rare golden-spined variant of the standard fishhook barrel that was found in the wild has been bred and propagated in Tucson by Chris Monrad of the Tucson Cactus and Succulent Society.

ATTRACTIVE IN SPINE AND FLOWER, THIS FISHHOOK BARREL IS COMING INTO AUGUST BLOOM IN SOUTHERN ARIZONA'S ALTAR VALLEY.

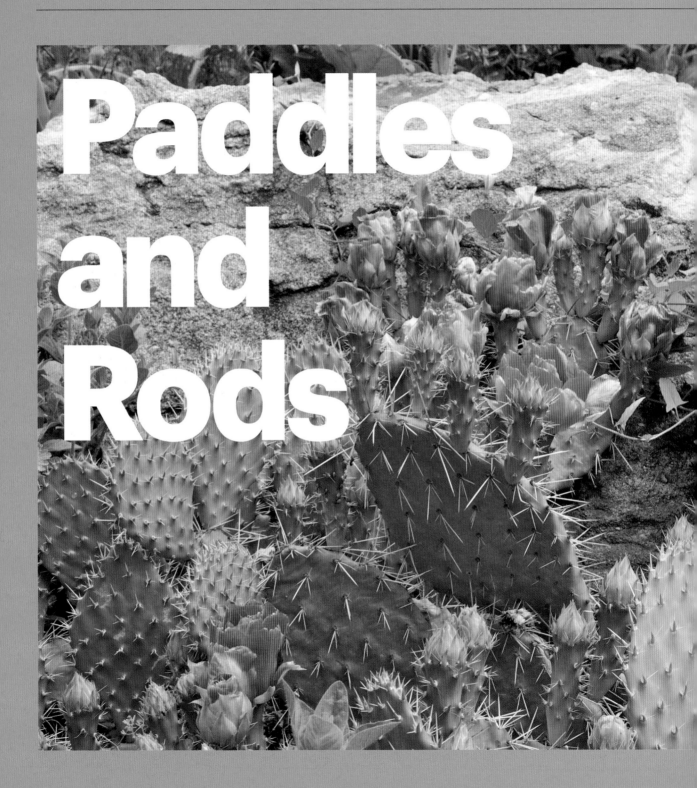

Paddles and Rods

THIS GROUP INCLUDES CACTUS WITH segmented parts, usually in the form of rounded pads (such as prickly pear—*Opuntia*) or cylindrical rods (such as cholla—*Cylindropuntia*). Plants in this group are some of the most cold-hardy and widely adaptable in the entire cactus family. They are known for their interesting forms, colorful flesh, flamboyant flowers, and edible fruit and pads. They are highly undervalued as garden plants. There is scarcely a region of the country where some species of prickly pear or cholla-type cactus cannot be grown successfully in the ground.

A BUSHEL OF NEW PRICKLY PEAR HYBRIDS, LIKE THIS *OPUNTIA* 'MALPAIS SUNSET', MAKES INTRODUCING AND COLLECTING NEW VARIETIES FUN AND REWARDING.

THE COLORFUL AND HIGHLY VARIABLE BLOOMS OF CHOLLA ADD INTEREST.

CHOLLAS LIKE THIS RED CHOLLA (CYLINDROPUNTIA ×CAMPII) GLOW WHEN BACKLIT.

► Plants in the genus *Cylindropuntia*—popularly known as cholla (pronounced choy-ya) have cylindrical rod-shaped stem segments and many species branch into small-scale, tree-like specimens. They are exceptionally spiny and are known to be difficult to handle, but they also have their landscape virtues. In garden settings, they are among the most striking plants, especially in situations where early or late light backlights the plant. Tall, segmented cholla stems catch light in their spines. The stems also make excellent bird habitat—they are the preferred nesting habitat for the cactus wren. Cholla flowers can be yellow, orange, russet, pink, or red. Native Americans roasted cholla buds and ate them as a vegetable; some contemporary gardeners pickle the cholla fruit.

Cholla look good planted near the top of berms and contours, paired with other low-water-use plants that complement their upright branch structure. Consider planting cholla alongside flattop buckwheat (*Eriogonum fasciculatum*), Apache plume (*Fallugia paradoxa*), gopher plant (*Euphorbia rigida*), giant purple-flowered ornamental onion (*Allium aflatunense* 'Purple Sensation'), and three-leaf sumac (*Rhus trilobata*). Planting wildflowers by seed around cholla cactus is also effective.

COLORFUL WHIPPLE'S CHOLLA IN SPRING BLOOM IN ANZA-BORREGO DESERT STATE PARK.

SNOW LEOPARD CHOLLA INTERPLANTED WITH TWO
BULBS: GIANT ALLIUM AND FOXTAIL LILY.

Chollas by Choice

The thin and sparely thorned stems of the pencil cholla suggest its common name. It is one of the more compact of the cholla plants, with pretty stems and flowers.

Cylindropuntia arbuscula
(Also sold as *Opuntia arbuscula*)

pencil cholla

NATIVE HABITAT	MATURE SIZE	HARDINESS	FLOWERING SEASON
Much of the Sonoran Desert, from central Arizona to central Sonora, Mexico	Up to 6 feet (1.8 m) tall and 3–6 feet (0.9–1.8 m) across	Zone 8b	Mid- to late spring

► Pencil cholla has a compact crown and is characterized by its many branches and smooth stem texture. Its thin stems are only 1/2 inch (1.3 cm) in diameter. The only plant in the cholla family with thinner stems is the desert Christmas cholla. The pencil cholla can develop a thick standard trunk with age and is also much taller in stature than the desert Christmas cholla. In addition to its attractive stems, its flowers are interesting shades of yellow-green to reddish brown. Like many chollas, its green, club-shaped fruit persists on the plant for many months. It typically grows in plains, valleys, and near washes.

DESIGN SUGGESTIONS

Because it is one of the less thorny chollas, pencil cholla can be placed in beds or planters somewhat near walkways. As with most of the chollas, it looks great incorporated into naturalistic desert plantings.

CULTIVATION

Pencil cholla is not particular about soil conditions and is tolerant of both summer and winter moisture. It is one of a few chollas that propagate themselves through their stems rather than by seed. For this reason, it is dead-simple to grow from a stem segment—just stick in well-drained soil and wait.

THE PENCIL CHOLLA SHOWS OFF ITS ATTRACTIVE BLOOMS AND SVELTE STEMS IN A PHOENIX GARDEN.

TEDDY BEAR CACTUS ON THE FLANKS OF PICACHO PEAK IN ARIZONA, GROWING WITH MEXICAN GOLD POPPY AND LUPINE.

The dense, almost furry, gold spines of the teddy bear cactus give it a stuffed animal look, but make no mistake—it might be loveable, but it is far from huggable.

Cylindropuntia bigelovii
(Also sold as *Opuntia bigelovii*)

teddy bear cactus

NATIVE HABITAT
Widespread throughout the Sonoran Desert including Arizona, California, Northern Baja California, and Sonora, Mexico

MATURE SIZE
Up to 6 feet (1.8 m) tall and 2–4 feet (0.6–1.2 m) across

HARDINESS
Zone 8

FLOWERING SEASON
Early spring to early summer and sometimes early autumn

► A spectacular plant in nature that is little used in gardens, teddy bear cactus's golden spines glow in the sun. As the plant ages, the older spines form a chocolate-brown thatch along its trunk. It can be either tree-like or shrubby. In either case, the teddy bear cactus is notorious for attaching itself to the skin, socks, shoes, jeans, and t-shirts of passersby—in fact, this is how it reproduces. Because seeds of the plant are mostly infertile, it propagates itself by flinging (not literally, although it might seem like it) its joints onto passing animals and humans, who unwittingly move them to a location where they can take root away from the mother plant—vegetative reproduction. The reason this strategy works so well is that the spines are hooked and will dislodge from the mother plant at the slightest touch; thus, the plant's other common name of jumping cholla is apt hyperbole. From a landscape perspective, its dense, furry arms and glowing spines are the primary draw, although inconspicuous yellowish green flowers are produced in the spring.

CULINARY VALUE
Buds can be roasted and eaten

DESIGN SUGGESTIONS
Stunning on the fringes of a property where it can be backlit by the sun. Mix it with desert shrubs and perennials such as globe mallow (*Sphaeralcea ambigua*) and brittlebush (*Encelia farinosa*). Teddy bear cholla is a great habitat plant for birds that will often nest in its branches.

CULTIVATION
Handle with tongs and heavy leather gloves. To dislodge a segment that is stuck to you, use tweezers, tongs, or a wide-toothed comb.

Spectacular silver spines and
unrivaled drought tolerance make
the silver cholla a garden winner.

Cylindropuntia echinocarpa
(Also sold as *Opuntia echinocarpa*)

silver cholla

NATIVE HABITAT

Occurs over a wide elevation range, 200–6000
feet (60–1800 m), in the hottest, driest parts of
California, Arizona, and Nevada; Baja California
and Sonora, Mexico

MATURE SIZE

18 inches to 6 feet
(0.5–1.8 m) tall and
18 inches to 4 feet
(0.5–1.2 m) across

HARDINESS

Zone 5

FLOWERING SEASON

Early spring to
early summer

► Silver cholla grows in some of the hottest and
driest habitats of any cactus in North America.
To put this in context, it grows in Death Valley—
in some cases, where it might be the only perennial plant besides creosote bush that is able to
make a living there. Although it is surely a heat
master, its habitat also extends into the Great
Basin, giving it a lot of cold tolerance as well. Its
spines are covered in a yellow sheath that falls
off to reveal the white spines beneath. The flowers of the silver cholla are pale green or yellow-
green and sometimes have a maroon tinge.

CULINARY VALUE
None known

DESIGN SUGGESTIONS
Fetching in an oak grassland planting inter-
spersed with companions such as Apache plume
(*Fallugia paradoxa*)

CULTIVATION
Silver cholla is adaptable to most growing conditions, so long as the soil is reasonably well
drained.

SILVER CHOLLA
SHINES AT
DENVER BOTANIC
GARDENS.

Cylindropuntia imbricata
(Also sold as *Opuntia imbricata*)

tree cholla

Thick green stems, excellent cold hardiness, and generous dark pink flowers make tree cholla a standout member of the genus.

NATIVE HABITAT	**MATURE SIZE**	**HARDINESS**	**FLOWERING SEASON**
Colorado, New Mexico, south-central U.S., and northern Mexico	To 9 feet (2.7 m) high and sprawling as wide as 6 feet (1.8 m)	Zone 5	Midspring to early summer, sometimes with a repeat bloom in late summer

► Tree cholla is one of the largest plants in its genus and specimens can top 9 feet in height. Growing up to 1 foot (30 cm) a year, it can achieve significant height in short order. Tree cholla is common on the southern Great Plains and in short-grass prairies where it is often both common and prolific. Its stems and fruit have prominent tubercles and are comparatively lightly spined so the handsome green flesh of the plant is more visible. Tree cholla has flowers that open during the day and close at night. Each flower opens only once, but the plant produces them so prolifically that it will be in bloom for many weeks.

CULINARY VALUE
Edible fruit and sap that is sometimes chewed as a gum

DESIGN SUGGESTIONS
This cactus makes an excellent security barrier up against earth-tone colored walls, which have the added benefit of making its flowers "pop."

CULTIVATION
Tree cholla's quick growth makes it a great plant to grow from transplanted segments.

NOTABLE VARIETIES, FORMS, AND SUBSPECIES
Several interesting forms have been selected: 'Fred's Red', a red-flowered form; 'Giant Form', a vigorous tall plant with exceptionally thick stems; and 'White Tower', a form whose white flowers have green centers.

A LARGE TREE CHOLLA IN THE BARNETT HOME GARDEN, PUEBLO, COLORADO.

Cylindropuntia ramosissima
(Also sold as *Opuntia ramosissima*)

diamond cholla

Diamond cholla is desirable for its slender blue-green stems, and super-long spines.

NATIVE HABITAT

The Mojave and Sonoran deserts at elevations up to 4000 feet (1219 m)

MATURE SIZE

18–78 inches (45–200 cm) tall and from 12–72 inches (30–185 cm) wide; in garden settings, most plants will not reach 36 inches (91 cm) tall

HARDINESS

Zone 7

FLOWERING SEASON

Mid- to late summer

A MASS PLANTING OF DIAMOND CHOLLA AT THE DESERT BOTANICAL GARDEN IN PHOENIX, ARIZONA.

► The diamond cholla is, pardon the pun, a gem of a cholla that seldom gets used in gardens. Ultra-long spines that grow at a 90° angle punctuate its delicate-looking blue-green stems. The effect can be magical and in early or late light the spines appear to sparkle. The spines are white and covered with a yellow paper-like sheath that gives them a two-tone appearance. A group of diamond cholla planted together has a horizontal aspect because of the way the spines extend out parallel to the ground. The skin of the plant has interesting, scale-like markings. Because diamond cholla is not a reliable bloomer, it is definitely a plant to grow for the spines rather than the flowers. However, when it blooms its flowers are often peach to orange.

DESIGN SUGGESTIONS

Excellent when grouped in masses, especially where low light will penetrate and illuminate their wonderful spines. One of the few cholla with a small enough stature to fit nicely in large containers.

CULTIVATION

Because they tend to grow in areas with alluvial soils, make sure to plant in a fast-draining soil.

At the risk of damning with faint praise, cane cholla has a somewhat tidier appearance than most in the genus. Plus, it is a great bird-nesting plant with handsome flowers and fruit.

Cylindropuntia spinosior
(Also sold as *Opuntia spinosior*)

cane cholla

NATIVE HABITAT	MATURE SIZE	HARDINESS	FLOWERING SEASON
Arizona and New Mexico, extending into northeastern Sonora and northwestern Chihuahua	7–10 feet (2.1–3 m) tall and 3–6 feet (.9–1.8 m) across	Zone 6	Midspring to early summer

► Cane cholla grows at higher elevations than most members of the genus. It is found in grasslands, mixed with oaks and pines at elevations up to 8100 feet (2469 m). Cane cholla gets its common name from its woody inner skeleton, often used by the desert travelers as a walking stick. In winter, some of the plant's stems droop and the color of the flesh turns a rich purple that highlights the plant's yellow fruit. Its flowers range from magenta (most common) to yellow, orange, brown, and red. The yellow fruit that follow often persist on the plant for an entire year, including while the plant is blooming, adding to the visual appeal.

CULINARY VALUE

Buds can be eaten and are often roasted and pickled.

DESIGN SUGGESTIONS

Good as either the centerpiece of a cactus garden (perhaps set up on a mound in the middle of a bed) or as a sort of hedging plant out on the perimeter of the garden. As with most chollas, it also make an excellent security deterrent when planted below windows.

CULTIVATION

Other than providing occasional summer watering to speed growth, no special care is required.

NOTABLE VARIETIES, FORMS, AND SUBSPECIES

Sean Hogan at Cistus Nursery has selected the highest elevation form from southeast Arizona's Pinaleño Mountains, where he found it growing at 8100 feet (2430 m). This selection has silver spines and cherry red flowers.

CANE CHOLLA IN SIMULTANEOUS FRUIT AND FLOWER GRACE THE ENTRY OF A TUCSON DEVELOPMENT.

Cylindropuntia versicolor
(Also sold as *Opuntia versicolor*)

staghorn cholla

Staghorn cholla is a big tree-like plant with high cold tolerance and particularly striking purple winter color.

NATIVE HABITAT	MATURE SIZE	HARDINESS	FLOWERING SEASON
Central Arizona and northern Sonora, Mexico	6–12 feet (1.8–3.6 m) tall and up to 6 feet (1.8 m) or more in width	Zone 7	Early to late spring

► This large, branching cholla takes on a deep purple or maroon color when stressed by drought or cold, giving it uncommon winter interest. It grows on slopes and in valleys in the Sonoran Desert but is also found in low elevation oak woodlands. As the second half of its botanical name hints, its flowers vary widely in color: they may be yellow-green or yellow, red, bronze, or purple. Like its relative cane cholla, it is also excellent bird-nesting habitat.

CULINARY VALUE
Fruit remains fleshy for many months and can be pickled.

DESIGN SUGGESTIONS
These are superb bird plants—several species including wrens will use staghorn cholla as nesting habitat. Great near entry monuments, or arranged in the landscape a safe distance from walkways.

CULTIVATION
The staghorn cholla appreciates a reasonably fast-draining soil but is not particular about much else.

STAGHORN CHOLLA IN HABITAT IN THE RINCON MOUNTAINS EAST OF TUCSON.

Latin name: *Cylindropuntia whipplei*
(Trade synonym: *Opuntia whipplei*)

whipple cholla; snow leopard

Thanks to excellent cold tolerance and the handsome appearance of named selections such as 'Snow Leopard,' whipple cholla might be the most sought-after garden cholla.

NATIVE HABITAT

Between 5000–7400 feet (1524–2255 m) in Arizona, Colorado, New Mexico, and Utah

MATURE SIZE

1–4 feet (30–120 cm) tall and 2–3 feet (60–91 cm) across

HARDINESS

Zone 5

FLOWERING SEASON

Late spring to early summer

► Much more compact than most other chollas, whipple cholla is a choice garden specimen. Growing not only in upper-elevation deserts, but also among sagebrush and pine forests, it has solid cold–hardiness. In appearance, it is highly variable. Most of the selections chosen for garden cultivation are densely covered in glassine-white spines that glow when backlit. Plants in the trade might be confused with silver cholla, but whipple cholla can be distinguished by its bumpy yellow fruit. In addition, whipple cholla branches in whorls. Its beautiful, clear, yellow-green flowers contrast brilliantly with its white spines. Along with *Opuntia imbricata* and *Opuntia spinosior*, whipple cholla forms a trinity of cold-hardy species for high elevation gardens.

CULINARY VALUE

The roots of whipple cholla are used medicinally.

DESIGN SUGGESTIONS

Excellent integrated into a garden filled with drought-tolerant perennials and bulbs. Place at the back of a bed, or use as a space divider at the top of a mound.

CULTIVATION

Easy; in the hottest desert locations, provide supplemental water over the hot summer months.

NOTABLE VARIETIES, FORMS, AND SUBSPECIES

Perhaps the most stunning of all the garden cholla, *Cylindropuntia whipplei* 'Snow Leopard' is highly prized. This selection comes from Don Campbell in Grand Junction, Colorado. Its spines are so white that they nearly glow in the dark.

CYLINDROPUNTIA WHIPPLEI 'SNOW LEOPARD' GROWING IN THE CHINLE CHAPTER OF THE CACTUS AND SUCCULENT SOCIETY OF AMERICA'S XERIC GARDEN IN GRAND JUNCTION, COLORADO.

BEAVERTAIL PRICKLY PEAR AND
MEXICAN GOLD POPPY STEAL THE SHOW
WHEN THEY BLOOM SYNCHRONOUSLY.

SEVERAL SPECIES OF PRICKLY PEARS ARE
AMONG THE VERY BEST FOR INTEGRATING INTO
NATURALISTIC PRAIRIE PLANTINGS.

PURPLE PRICKLY PEAR USED TO
ITS FULL ADVANTAGE IN A
RESIDENTIAL FRONT YARD.

▶ From the prairie to the seashore to the mountains, prickly pear cactus have made a run of the country and occur naturally in nearly every state in the nation and across North America. This extraordinary adaptability makes for a rich diversity of garden plants. For landscapes they come in a surfeit of sizes and colors; consider the low-growing plains prickly pear, the shrub-sized purple prickly pear, or the massive tree-like Indian fig. All in all, they make for great low-water-use sculptural plants in gardens, with the added benefit—which should not be pooh-poohed—of having edible fruit and pads. Preceding the fruit, nearly all of the prickly pear varieties have showy flowers in various shades of yellow, orange, red, or pink.

There are many perennial flowers that are excellent for growing in combination with prickly pears. To complement prickly pear plants with purple or pink pads and/or flowers, consider Angelita daisy (*Tetraneuris acaulis*), damianita daisy (*Chrysactinia mexicana*), and paper flower (*Psilostrophe tagetina*). Other plants that work well include rock penstemon (*Penste-*

THE ABUNDANT AND FLAVORFUL FRUIT ON ENGELMANN'S PRICKLY PEAR CAN BE USED TO MAKE A MAGENTA-COLORED LEMONADE OR MARGARITA.

PLACING POTTED CACTUS INTO THE MIDDLE OF GARDEN BEDS CREATES A SCULPTURAL CENTERPIECE.

Prickly Pear Passion

mon *baccharifolius*), sand penstemon (*Penstemon ambiguous*), and firecracker penstemon (*Penstemon eatonii*). For prickly pear plantings in meadow or prairie-themed gardens, try planting prickly pear among grasses such as blue grama (*Bouteloua gracilis*) and sideoats grama (*Bouteloua curtipendula*).

Opuntia aurea 'Coombe's Winter Glow'

winter glow beavertail

One of the very best ornamental prickly pears for high elevation cities, winter glow beavertail's pads turn merlot red in winter.

NATIVE HABITAT	MATURE SIZE	HARDINESS	FLOWERING SEASON
Utah	8 inches (20 cm) high and up to 5 feet (1.5 m) across	Zone 5	Early summer

WINTER GLOW BEAVERTAIL THRIVING IN A BED AT TIMBERLINE GARDENS IN THE DENVER AREA.

► The exceptionally handsome, smooth, spineless pads and ruffled pink flowers set the winter glow beavertail apart; combine these traits with its exceptionally dark purple-red winter appearance and you can see the garden potential of the plant. It is a low grower whose pads will spread slowly to form a short, 5-foot-diameter (1.5 m) clump. Exceptional in rock gardens or intermixed with other landscape plants. Its transition from fall to winter is interesting; its pads begin to blush pink, then progress to a deep wine red as winter arrives.

DESIGN SUGGESTIONS

Plant on rocky slopes—mixed with native western shrubs such as cliffrose (*Purshia mexicana*)—or even with traditional landscape groundcovers such as creeping juniper.

CULTIVATION

Keep the plant tidy by removing the fruit in late summer, before their seeds fully ripen and fall to the ground. Cooking tongs are a great tool for this chore.

Opuntia basilaris

beavertail cactus

With its glowing dark pink flowers, blue-green pads, and relative spinelessness, it is easy to see why the beavertail is a garden favorite.

NATIVE HABITAT

California's Mojave Desert, east into Nevada and Arizona, Utah; Sonora, Mexico

MATURE SIZE

To 20 inches (51 cm) high and up to 6 feet (1.8 m) across

HARDINESS

Zone 5

FLOWERING SEASON

Late winter to early summer

► One of the most adaptable of all prickly pear cactus, it has been known to withstand summer temperatures over 122° F (50° C) as well as zone 5 winter lows. The pads of the beavertail, while predominantly blue-green, often take on a purplish tint during drought or cold weather. The plant is low-growing and forms dense clumps than can spread to widths over 6 feet wide. The flowers are a deep cherry pink and some of them are known to have a sweet watermelon-like fragrance. There are several subspecies and selected varieties of beavertail cactus, including the handsome compact subspecies, short-joint beavertail (*Opuntia basilaris* subsp. *brachylada*). Within the beavertail's expansive range, it is found in a variety of habitats including rocky slopes, low creosote flats, as well as juniper flats.

DESIGN SUGGESTIONS

Its low growth and handsome flowers recommend beavertail for prominent placement in xeric front-garden landscaping. Try mixing it with the perennial Angelita daisy (*Tetraneuris acaulis*) for a pink/yellow combination. It is also handsome paired with compass barrel cactus.

CULTIVATION

In habitat it grows in granitic soils. Try incorporating decomposed granite into your potting mix or simply top-dressing the pot with washed granite gravel.

NOTABLE VARIETIES, FORMS, AND SUBSPECIES

The dwarf subspecies, short-joint beavertail (*Opuntia basilaris* subsp. *brachylada*), is a nice compact choice, as is the selection *Opuntia basilaris* 'Sara's Compact'. Both of these smaller forms rarely exceed 18 inches (45 cm) in height. For orange flowers, *Opuntia basilaris* 'Peachy' is the best choice.

A BLOOMING BEAVERTAIL SPECIMEN PERCHED ON A GRANITE SLOPE IN ANZA-BORREGO NATIONAL PARK, CALIFORNIA, IN LATE MARCH.

BABY RITA IN FULL SPLENDOR AT BACH'S CACTUS NURSERY IN TUCSON.

This hybrid inherits added cold tolerance, pink flowers, and compact stature from its beavertail parent; purple pads and vigor from its Santa Rita side. All around, it is a winner of a garden plant.

Opuntia basilaris × O. santa-rita
(Also sold as *Opuntia santa-rita × O. basilaris*)

Baby Rita

NATIVE HABITAT

Because Baby Rita is a hybrid of two prickly pears whose native ranges don't naturally intersect, it doesn't have a traditional native habitat

MATURE SIZE

Less than 24 inches (60 cm) tall and 24–48 inches (60–120 cm) across

HARDINESS

Zone 6

FLOWERING SEASON

Early to late spring

► If seen when out of bloom, at first glance, it might be mistaken for a regular Santa Rita prickly pear. In bloom, its profusion of ruffled pink flowers leaves no doubt that it is something different. If you pay attention, you'll also notice that Baby Rita is considerably smaller than a straight Santa Rita, growing less than 2 feet (60 cm) high. Its pads are also smaller and emerge blue-green, sometimes tinged with pink.

DESIGN SUGGESTIONS

Excellent in mass plantings or adjacent to green-trunked trees such as palo verde species; also a fine container or rock garden plant

CULTIVATION

Baby Rita is easy to propagate from pads; grow in full sun and provide sharp drainage.

NOTABLE VARIETIES, FORMS, AND SUBSPECIES

Cistus Nursery in Portland sells a wonderful small plant as *Opuntia santa-rita × O. basilaris* 'Baby Rita'.

A tenacious grower with handsome gray-green pads, showy flowers, and abundant edible fruit.

Opuntia engelmannii

Engelmann's prickly pear

NATIVE HABITAT

Native across a wide swath of the Southwest, from California to Texas and from northern Mexico to Utah

MATURE SIZE

Up to 6 feet high (1.8 m) and up to 10 feet (3 m) across, although often much smaller in garden situations

HARDINESS

Zone 7

FLOWERING SEASON

Mid- to late spring

▶ Engelmann's prickly pear is a workhorse of a garden cactus. Its proportions might seem daunting—it can get as tall as a man and sprawl to a width of 10 feet—but in real garden situations it is often much smaller, and a little pad pruning every couple of years keeps it at a nice size of 3 feet high and 4 feet wide. Engelmann's prickly pear has pads that are a pleasing gray-green or sometimes blue-green color, and flowers that range from yellow (most common) to peachy oranges; in fact, even the yellow flowers fade to a pleasing light orange on the second day after they open. Its spines are a two-tone red and white, and after flowering it produces juicy, dark red fruit (known as *tunas*) with magenta flesh that are commonly eaten in the Southwest. When Engelmann's prickly pear grows new pads, they are glossy lime-green, thornless, and pliable before becoming stout, fibrous, dull, and thorny with maturity.

CULINARY VALUE

Fruit has a tasty pulp and juice, with proven health benefits for diabetics. The juice is used to make delicious magenta-colored jelly, lemonade, margaritas, and marinades for meat.

DESIGN SUGGESTIONS

Plant adjacent to workhorse shrubs such as autumn amber sumac (*Rhus trilobata* 'Autumn Amber') and Apache plume (*Fallugia paradoxa*), or next to tough perennials such as Mexican blue sage (*Salvia chamaedryoides*), giant-flowered purple sage (*Salvia pachyphylla*), and firewheel (*Gaillardia pulchella*).

CULTIVATION

Every 2–4 years, control overvigorous growth by pruning off pads—this is easily done with a shovel.

NOTABLE VARIETIES, FORMS, AND SUBSPECIES

Opuntia engelmannii subsp. *flavispina* has yellow, rather than white and red, spines.

ENGELMANN'S PRICKLY PEAR LADEN WITH FRUIT IN AN ALBUQUERQUE GARDEN DESIGNED BY JUDITH PHILLIPS.

Opuntia engelmannii subsp. *lindheimeri*
(Also sold as *Opuntia lindheimeri*)

Texas prickly pear

With her scarlet-to-orange flowers, Texas prickly pear is like the wild big sister of Engelmann's prickly pear.

NATIVE HABITAT

Mostly east of the Pecos river in Texas, as well as Oklahoma, New Mexico, and Southwest Louisiana

MATURE SIZE

3–6 feet (0.9–1.8 m) tall and up to 8 feet (2.4 m) across, although typically smaller in garden conditions

HARDINESS

Zone 6

FLOWERING SEASON

Late spring to early summer

► This subspecies of Engelmann's prickly pear is chosen mostly for its flashy red or red-orange flowers. It flowers prolifically and some individuals have deep fruit-punch-red flowers. Although in habitat the majority of Texas prickly pears are yellow-flowered, selections in the nursery trade are almost uniformly red- or orange-flowered. Texas prickly pear differs from regular Engelmann's in that it has yellow spines and tends to have more and longer golden glochids. It also has fewer long spines per areole (little dot-like eyes on the pads). Its native range extends much further east than regular Engelmann's prickly pear, suggesting that it might be more tolerant of extra moisture.

CULINARY VALUE

Like regular Engelmann's prickly pear, the young, spineless pads can be cooked as a vegetable; the juice and pulp from the fruit is used in jams, jellies, syrups, drinks, and candies.

DESIGN SUGGESTIONS

Excellent when used along a pathway (taking care to allow for their mature size), where their fruit-punch-colored blooms add showstopping zip to a border. Also good as a back-of-the-border plant in a cactus garden.

CULTIVATION

Plants with provenance in southwestern Louisiana have good tolerance of wet conditions.

TEXAS PRICKLY PEAR BLOOMING AGAINST A STONE WALL IN THE CHIHUAHUAN DESERT GARDENS IN EL PASO, TEXAS.

Opuntia engelmannii subsp. *linguiformis*
(Also sold as *Opuntia linguiformis*)

cow's tongue prickly pear

The elongated pads and tall stature of cow's tongue prickly pear make it an interesting focal point for gardens.

NATIVE HABITAT

Thought to be from central Texas, although cow's tongue prickly pear has naturalized in many places in the Southwest

MATURE SIZE

Usually 6–10 feet high (1.8–3 m) tall and not quite as wide

HARDINESS

Zone 7b

FLOWERING SEASON

Late spring to early summer

► Although it is a subspecies of Engelmann's prickly pear, this cactus hardly resembles its close cousin. Cow's tongue prickly pear's main landscape assets are its upright nature and spectacularly elongated, blue-green colored pads, which can exceed 2 feet (60 cm) in length. The form of the plant is so different from other prickly pear cactus that it is instantly recognizable. It is thought to come from central Texas, although nobody knows for sure because the plant has been so widely traded in nurseries for many years and has naturalized outside of its native range; in fact, it may be extinct in its native range. Cow's tongue prickly is thought to be a variation of plain Texas prickly pear and occasionally its pads will revert to a more ovoid shape. Cow's tongue is an oddity in that it grows to an indeterminate size. That is, its ultimate height and width depend on the conditions in which it is grown rather that a limiting genetic factor.

CULINARY VALUE

Like Engelmann's prickly pear, the fruit is tasty and has a tart, melon flavor. It is fine for all of the same culinary uses as Engelmann's.

DESIGN SUGGESTIONS

This is a great plant to use as an anchor at the corner of a house or against a wall where you need a tall, sculptural plant. It looks good planted with Mormon tea (*Ephedra nevadensis*).

CULTIVATION

In prolonged extreme cold or drought, large segments may topple. Prevent by covering with frost cloth or by watering in extremely dry conditions.

A MATURE COW'S TONGUE PRICKLY PEAR ADDS SCULPTURAL FORM BESIDE A FRONT PORCH.

INDIAN FIG
PLANTED UP
AGAINST A
COLORED WALL
IN TUCSON'S
BARRIO VIEJO
NEIGHBORHOOD.

Probably the most cultivated cactus in the world, the Indian fig is the big kahuna of trunk-forming, edible cactus. Its fat, green pads recommend it as a landscape plant.

Opuntia ficus-indica

Indian fig

NATIVE HABITAT

Unknown, but thought to be from central Mexico; it has naturalized in the Mediterranean, South Africa, and Australia

MATURE SIZE

3.3–20 feet (1–6 m) tall with a trunk up to 14 inches in diameter (35 cm)

HARDINESS

Zone 9

FLOWERING SEASON

Spring to summer

► Thick, green, oval-shaped spineless pads and a vigorous upright stature distinguish this excellent garden prickly pear. Beyond its ornamental attributes, it is an important food plant in much of the warm-winter world. In Mexico, its young pads are harvested, cooked, and used as the vegetable *nopales*, which tastes something akin to green beans. The fruit, or *tunas*, are also used extensively in Mexico and available at midsummer roadside stands throughout that country. *Tunas* are sometimes sold mixed in a smoothie with pineapple juice. A bonus to growing the Indian fig is that its spineless pads have few irritating glochids. Indian fig has been cultivated and fiddled with for many years. It was one of the first (maybe *the* first) prickly pear imported to Europe. It has yellow to red flowers and the fruit that follows can be green, orange (most common), or red. The great California plantsman Luther Burbank did much hybridizing with Indian fig, trying to create a plant suitable for cattle forage. Although that effort is counted as one of Burbank's failures (Indian figs are one of the more thirsty of the prickly pears), he did produce several cultivars that are still traded today.

CULINARY VALUE

Excellent pads and fruit. New pads need to be scraped of any glochids and can be sautéed in olive oil. The ripe fruit is excellent juiced and imparts a melon-like flavor.

DESIGN SUGGESTIONS

Commonly used as a hedge in the Southwest, they make a handsome living fence if properly maintained.

CULTIVATION

Indian figs need more regular watering during the warm months than most other cactus species, especially if you are growing them for fruit and pad production. They also will tend to collapse or fall down during extended below-freezing weather, so place and protect accordingly.

NOTABLE VARIETIES, FORMS, AND SUBSPECIES

Luther Burbank's Indian fig cultivars were poorly documented, but Brad Lancaster in Tucson claims to have two tasty Burbank hybrids: *Opuntia ficus-indica* 'Sicilian Port Wine' and *O. ficus-indica* 'Dreamsicle', both of which bear fruit that taste like their names. Other worthwhile selections in the trade include *O. ficus-indica* 'Lynnwood' and *O. ficus-indica* 'Santa Ynez'.

**POTATO CACTUS
HAPPILY CREEPING
ACROSS A ROCKY
BED IN GRAND JUNC-
TION, COLORADO.**

The charming little potato cactus is more cold hardy than any other species of cactus. It is a spineless low-grower with pads shaped like potatoes and will grow quickly to form a mat.

Opuntia fragilis forma denudata
(Also sold as *Opuntia schweriniana*)

potato cactus

NATIVE HABITAT

Common in the cooler parts of the midwestern United States, and as far north as the southern portion of the Canadian Northwest Territory

MATURE SIZE

4–8 inches (10–20 cm) high and from 10 inches to 6 feet wide (25 cm–1.8 m)

HARDINESS

Zone 3

FLOWERING SEASON

Late spring

▶ The most northerly growing species of cactus, its habitat ranges well into Canada. As its namesake suggests, its pads resemble plump new potatoes. As cold temperatures arrive, the pads take on a purple-red hue not unlike red potatoes. Their pleasant shape and lack of long thorns make potato cactus a garden winner. Although the form shown here, *denudata*, meaning "naked," appears to be bald, the potato cactus is not wholly unarmed—it still has hairlike glochids that can irritate your skin. Potato cactus is shy to flower—if it does they are pink or yellow—but the real draw is the interesting pad shape.

DESIGN SUGGESTIONS

Excellent for covering ground on dry slopes, or for providing an interesting textural mat near a walkway. One of the few cactus that can form a weed-blocking barrier.

CULTIVATION

Best for cooler regions. Suffers in the heat of the low deserts. Take care to plant in locations where its roots won't sit in standing water over the winter months.

NOTABLE VARIETIES, FORMS, AND SUBSPECIES

Many interesting dwarf forms are in the market. One form, 'Dwarf Golden' from Denver plantsman Panayoti Kelaidis, grows to only 4 inches (10 cm) tall and 18 inches (45 cm) wide and has glowing golden spines. Another form from Sean Hogan at Cistus Nursery in Portland, Oregon, has chartreuse yellow flowers and because of its provenance near Ashland, Oregon, can withstand significant winter moisture without rotting.

Distinct, low-growing, intensely purple pads make this plant a miniature version of its larger cousin, the purple prickly pear. Unlike that plant, milk-chocolate spine prickly pear has handsome brown spines.

Opuntia gosseliniana
(Also sold as *Opuntia violacea* var. *gosseliniana*)

milk-chocolate spine prickly pear

NATIVE HABITAT	MATURE SIZE	HARDINESS	FLOWERING SEASON
Arizona; Baja California, Sonora, and Chihuahua, Mexico	Usually less than 24 inches (60 cm) tall and across	Zone 9	Late spring to midsummer

► Known for its small, dark purple or purple-red pads that keep their color for most of the year. The pads of milk-chocolate spine prickly pear are smaller—less than 8 inches (20 cm) across—than most other purple prickly pears and are often clustered tightly together lending a compact, orderly appearance. Some selections of this plant are spineless, but the most desired and common in the trade have the characteristic long brownish red- to rust-colored spines. Yellow flowers appear reluctantly in cultivation, but the real draw is the purple stem color and brown spines.

DESIGN SUGGESTIONS

This low-growing cactus is stunning planted among yellow-flowered xeric ground covers such as shrubby dogweed (*Thymophylla pentachaeta*) and sierra gold dalea (*Dalea capitata*). A good candidate for hell-strip plantings.

CULTIVATION

For best pad coloration, grow milk-chocolate spine in full, strong sunlight.

MILK-CHOCOLATE SPINE PRICKLY PEAR TURNING AUTUMN PURPLE IN A TUCSON, ARIZONA, GARDEN.

Opuntia humifusa
(Also sold as *Opuntia compressa* var. *humifusa*)

eastern prickly pear

A great ground cover plant where you want a Gumby-green mat of plump ears. Eastern prickly pear is the best choice for those living east of the 100th meridian.

NATIVE HABITAT

Widespread across the eastern half of North America

MATURE SIZE

Less than 12 inches (30 cm) high and up to 24 inches (60 cm) across

HARDINESS

Zone 3

FLOWERING SEASON

Late winter to late summer

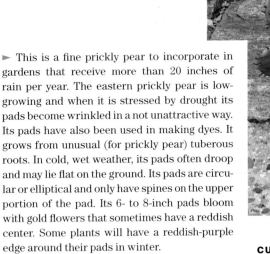

EASTERN PRICKLY PEAR GROWING IN A CUTOUT IN PERMEABLE STONE PAVING AT THE DELAWARE CENTER FOR HORTICULTURE.

► This is a fine prickly pear to incorporate in gardens that receive more than 20 inches of rain per year. The eastern prickly pear is low-growing and when it is stressed by drought its pads become wrinkled in a not unattractive way. Its pads have also been used in making dyes. It grows from unusual (for prickly pear) tuberous roots. In cold, wet weather, its pads often droop and may lie flat on the ground. Its pads are circular or elliptical and only have spines on the upper portion of the pad. Its 6- to 8-inch pads bloom with gold flowers that sometimes have a reddish center. Some plants will have a reddish-purple edge around their pads in winter.

DESIGN SUGGESTIONS

Excellent as a low maintenance ground cover, or used in a cascading fashion in rockwork; also can be planted in permeable paving stones as an interesting accent

CULTIVATION

Eastern prickly pear is not particular about growing conditions, but as with other species, avoid boggy situations. Don't give up on it in the winter, although it might collapse so flatly as to resemble roadkill. Wait until warm weather arrives to see it perk up.

Opuntia polyacantha

Plains prickly pear

A fantastic plant for gardens in the Great Plains and Midwest. It boasts extreme cold hardiness, a low-growing habit, and a wide range of selections mostly made for flower color; additionally, it mixes well with grasses and perennials.

NATIVE HABITAT

Widespread from extreme northern Mexico, throughout the western United States and into southern Canada

MATURE SIZE

Usually 6–10 inches (15–25 cm) high and as wide as 6 feet (1.8 m), but more typically in garden settings 24–36 inches (60–90 cm) across

HARDINESS

Zone 3

FLOWERING SEASON

Midspring to early summer

▶ Perhaps the most wide-ranging and horticulturally useful plant in the entire prickly pear cactus group, Plains prickly pear is found hunkered down in the short-grass prairie. It is a relatively short plant seldom topping 6 inches high (15 cm), but it can spread out in a wide mat that sometimes exceeds 6 feet (1.8 m) in diameter. Plains prickly pear has highly variable spine density and flower color. For this reason, there have been many selections made to single out plants with unusually colored flowers or especially hirsute spined pads. Because of this selection and breeding, the choice of named selections and cultivars is broad.

CULINARY VALUE

The sap (mucilage) from the pads of Plains prickly pear has been used to stabilize dyes in fabric.

DESIGN SUGGESTIONS

Excellent mixed with blue grama grass (*Bouteloua gracilis*) in a prairie theme, or used on its own as a small mat of ground cover. Depending on flower color, it mixes nicely with drought-tolerant perennials such as West Texas grass sage (*Salvia reptens*) and shimmer primrose (*Oenothera fremonti* 'Shimmer').

CULTIVATION

One of the most forgiving cactus, it will tolerate a wide range of soil types including reasonably well-drained clay. Best in full sun—also handsome growing among native grasses.

NOTABLE VARIETIES, FORMS, AND SUBSPECIES

Opuntia polyacantha subsp. *erinacea* is treated as a separate entry, but some other standout selections of *O. polyacantha* include 'Crystal Tide', 'Nebraska Orange', 'Pawnee's Deep Pink', 'Citrus Punch', and 'Goldmine'.

OPUNTIA POLYACANTHA 'CRYSTAL TIDE' THRIVING IN THE GARDENS AT KENDRICK LAKE IN LAKEWOOD, COLORADO.

Known for its long, hairlike spines that nearly obscure its pads, grizzly bear prickly pear is well represented in botanical gardens and nurseries throughout western North America.

Opuntia polyacantha subsp. *erinacea*
(Also sold as *Opuntia erinacea*;
Opuntia erinacea var. *ursina*; *Opuntia ursina*)

grizzly bear prickly pear; Mojave prickly pear

NATIVE HABITAT

The four-corners states—Utah, Colorado, Arizona, and New Mexico—as well as California and Nevada; from 3400 to 10,400 (1036–3170 m) feet in elevation

MATURE SIZE

To 20 inches (51 cm) high and up to 6 feet (1.8 m) across

HARDINESS

Zone 4

FLOWERING SEASON

Late spring to midsummer

▶ Distinctive hairiness sets the grizzly bear apart from other prickly pears. Its spines vary from 2 to 4 inches in length and are usually white. In the nursery trade these shaggy plants are often labeled as *Opuntia erinacea* var. *ursina* or *Opuntia ursina*. The longest spines are found on the lower and most senior pads on each plant. They typically bloom yellow although some populations have watermelon pink flowers. Grizzly bears have some of the best cold tolerance of any prickly pears and are as comfortable in Denver gardens as they are in Las Vegas.

DESIGN SUGGESTIONS

Superb as a focal point in a garden with fine-textured perennials, ornamental grasses, and succulents such as bear grass (*Nolina microcarpa*). Also handsome placed in an urn-shaped pot where backlighting will illuminate the hairy spines.

CULTIVATION

In cold winter climates, the plants may lay prostrate in winter, but will recover when warmer weather arrives.

GRIZZLY BEAR PRICKLY PEAR GROWING BENEATH A CLUMP OF BEAR GRASS (*NOLINA MICROCARPA*).

Opuntia phaeacantha 'Dark Knight'
(Also sold as *Opuntia* 'Dark Knight')

dark knight prickly pear

If you have visited southern Arizona during the winter and have fallen in love with a purple prickly pear (such as *Opuntia santarita*) that is not cold hardy in your climate, dark knight is a fine substitute and a good way to get your purple pad fix.

NATIVE HABITAT

Wide distribution throughout the southwestern United States and northern Mexico

MATURE SIZE

10 inches (25 cm) tall and up to 4 feet (1.2 m) across

HARDINESS

Zone 4

FLOWERING SEASON

Early summer

DARK KNIGHT BLOOMING IN JUNE AT TIMBERLINE GARDENS, ARVADA, COLORADO.

pink flowers is luscious. Midwinter, its pads approach black in color, which makes its white spines stand out all the more. It is a fairly large and robust plant and was originally selected by the great western plantsman Claude Barr.

DESIGN SUGGESTIONS

Striking when planted in mass

CULTIVATION

Dark knight is easy to grow in the ground in a wide section of North America, especially west of the Mississippi; in eastern locales, container culture is best.

► Its grape-juice-colored pads and white needles get you right away. Dark knight is a striking plant in winter, but it also holds its purple-red color well into early summer. This is notable because early summer is when its hot pink flowers appear and the contrast of the purple pad and

Opuntia 'Peter Pan'
(Also sold as *Opuntia polyacantha* 'Peter Pan')

Peter Pan prickly pear

A wonderful compact and symmetrical form discovered by Colorado plantsman Kelly Grummons.

NATIVE HABITAT	MATURE SIZE	HARDINESS	FLOWERING SEASON
Eastern Colorado	3 inches (8 cm) high and up to 24 inches (60 cm) across	Zone 3	Isn't known to flower

► Like the character it is named after, Peter Pan is in a state of arrested development. Botanically speaking, he never matures enough to flower. However, 'Peter Pan' does form an excellent white-spined mound that is uniform, small, and very cold hardy. 'Peter Pan' is most likely a form of *Opuntia polyacantha* and was discovered in Colorado's Pawnee National Grasslands by Kelly Grummons. It is an outstanding landscape plant whose petite size enables it to fit in tight garden spaces.

DESIGN SUGGESTIONS

The lovely little plant is great worked into a rock garden or with other drought-tolerant perennials. It is equally happy planted with native grasses in a prairie-themed garden.

CULTIVATION

'Peter Pan' is easy to grow, although the usual advice about avoiding waterlogged soils in winter applies. It is happiest planted north of the low deserts of the Southwest.

PETER PAN PRICKLY PEAR GROWING AMONG ANNUAL POPPIES IN A DENVER GARDEN.

Hefty pads that grow to the circumference of dinner plates characterize this large plant. It is also notable for its excellent fruit.

Opuntia robusta

dinner plate prickly pear; clock-face prickly pear

NATIVE HABITAT	**MATURE SIZE**	**HARDINESS**	**FLOWERING SEASON**
Native to Mexico, from Hidalgo and Michoacán north to Chihuahua and eastern Sonora	3–10 feet (0.9–3 m) tall and 3–6 feet (0.9–1.8 m) across	Zone 8b	Midsummer to early autumn

► One of the largest of all the prickly pears, the dinner plate's pads reach a diameter of 18 inches (45 cm). The pads are thick and often have a dusty blue-green (glaucous) cast. Dinner plate prickly pear is a robust grower with a mostly upright habit. It has yellow flowers and the fruit that follow are huge tennis-ball-sized units that make for excellent eating. Dinner plate is slightly tricky to grow, as too much water on newly rooting (or not-quite-rooted) pads causes rotting; conversely, established plants are reluctant to bloom and set fruit with too little water. The northern forms of the plant grow among oak and pine forests at high elevations and can take significant cold temperatures.

CULINARY VALUE

Big, juicy magenta fruit with medium-sweet, melon-flavored juice

DESIGN SUGGESTIONS

Wonderful at the back of the border or used as a hedge, dinner plate is a spectacular specimen, sure to be appreciated by garden visitors.

CULTIVATION

Dinner plate pads tend to droop or fall off in weather below 20° F (−6.6 C). It also needs fast-draining soil for best fruit production. When propagating the plant from pads, water only sparingly and plant in fast-draining soil. Dinner plate prickly pear is more susceptible to rotting than other prickly pears.

NOTABLE VARIETIES, FORMS, AND SUBSPECIES

A variety bred for lack of spines, *Opuntia robusta* 'Spineless' has blue-green pads, extra-large fruit, and of course, fewer spines.

THE FRUIT OF THE DINNER PLATE IS
AS TASTY AS IT IS PRETTY.

DINNER PLATE PRICKLY PEAR FIGURES PROMINENTLY AT THE BACK OF THE BORDER IN THIS TUCSON GARDEN.

Tuna colorado is a distinctive and visually stunning prickly pear with purple markings like no other.

Opuntia stenopetala

tuna colorado; purple fishnet prickly pear

NATIVE HABITAT	MATURE SIZE	HARDINESS	FLOWERING SEASON
The northern Mexican states of Coahuila, Nuevo León, San Luis Potosí, and Tamaulipas	From 6–12 inches (15–30 cm) tall and 3–4 feet (0.9–1.2 m) across	Zone 8b	Late spring to midsummer

▶ Somehow, this fantastic prickly pear from the high Chihuahuan Desert has been overlooked as a landscape plant. Its aesthetic appeal really comes into play in the wintertime when its pads become crisscrossed or striped with purple. No other species has markings like this plant. Equally arresting are its flowers, which bloom in a fiery orange color. As they come into flower, red-orange horn-shaped protrusions sprout along the ridge of the pads. Flowers are unisexual. Tuna colorado's growth habit is sprawling and relatively low.

DESIGN SUGGESTIONS

Tuna colorado is great in a mass planting or interspersed with other plants such as fairy duster (*Calliandra* species), ocotillo (*Fouquieria splendens*), and *Thelocactus* species.

CULTIVATION

Because the level of purple coloration, pattern, and intensity vary from plant to plant, grow tuna colorado by pad cuttings from an especially handsome plant viewed in winter. The sexiest selections have strong purple fishnet markings on their pads.

THE FIERY FLOWER BUDS OF TUNA COLORADO THRIVE IN AN EL PASO, TEXAS, GARDEN.

TUNA COLORADO IN ITS PURPLE HIGH-WINTER COLORATION AT THE DESERT BOTANICAL GARDEN IN PHOENIX SURROUNDED BY PURPLE CHIHULY GLASS SCULPTURE.

Opuntia trichophora
(Also sold as *Opuntia polyacantha* var. *ursina*)

white grizzly prickly pear

As prickly pears with shaggy long spines go, none is hairier than white grizzly. Its small size and excellent cold hardiness also recommend it as a garden specimen.

NATIVE HABITAT

Extreme northern Chihuahua, Mexico; New Mexico, Utah, and in the Trans-Pecos region of Texas, north to Flaming Gorge in Wyoming

MATURE SIZE

To 12 inches (30 cm) high and to 36 inches (90 cm) or more across

HARDINESS

Zone 5

FLOWERING SEASON

Late spring to early summer

OPUNTIA TRICHOPHORA 'WHITE GRIZZLY' GROWING IN A POT AT SANTA FE GREENHOUSES, SANTA FE, NEW MEXICO.

▶ Remarkably hairy, particularly on its lower and older pads, white grizzly prickly pear makes its home near Santa Fe, New Mexico, where it was first discovered by railroad surveyors in 1857. It grows on volcanic rock faces and mesas among native grasses and pinyon pines. Its spines become long and flexible as they mature, and on the best garden selections the spines form a thick nest around the lower pads, often obscuring them completely. Spines on the new pads are sometimes shorter and stiffer. The spines are typically glassine white, but occasionally golden yellow. The flowers are yellow (and occasionally pink), fading to orange. Due to its adorable hairiness and relative cold tolerance, it is a plant that should find purchase in many more gardens. Its only drawback as a garden plant is its slow growth rate in relation to other prickly pears.

DESIGN SUGGESTIONS

Wonderful as a specimen sprawling out of an urn-shaped pot, white grizzly is equally arresting in a rock garden, or in hypertufa pots.

CULTIVATION

Although it is found growing in soils with some clay content, white grizzly seems to grow mostly in rocky volcanic soils. With this in mind, incorporating volcanic material such as scoria into the soil or potting mix will be rewarded.

NOTABLE VARIETIES, FORMS, AND SUBSPECIES

A handsome selection with long, pure-white spines, 'White Grizzly', is being propagated by Santa Fe plantsman David Salman.

Opuntia macrocentra subsp. *macrocentra*
(Also sold as *Opuntia violacea* var. *macrocentra*)

tuxedo spine prickly pear; long spine prickly pear

Arguably the most alluring of all of the purple-tinted prickly pears, the tuxedo spine boasts a floriferous nature, manageable stature, and slick-looking black and white spines.

NATIVE HABITAT	MATURE SIZE	HARDINESS	FLOWERING SEASON
Arizona, New Mexico, Texas; Sonora, Mexico	18–39 inches (45–100 cm) tall and to 4 feet (1.2 m) wide, often considerably smaller in cultivation	Zone 8b	Mid- to late spring

▶ A smaller and perhaps more interesting alternative to the more commonly planted purple prickly pear, the tuxedo spine has much to recommend it over its larger cousin. Its short stature is more appropriate for small garden spaces. Decorating its pads are some of the most distinctive spines found on any cactus: black spines with white tips. Its pads are a cool blue-green that tends to turn purple—especially along the edge of the pad—during drought or cold. It also differs from purple prickly pear in that it doesn't form a trunk like you would find on a mature purple prickly pear. Its flowers are a two-tone affair with blood-red centers and yellow to gold outer petals; after blooming, they often fade to an attractive peach color. They produce a bumper crop of flowers, especially on plants in cultivation. As with many prickly pears, there is some taxonomic confusion. Tucson horticulturalist Matt Johnson remarks that many plants sold in Nurseries as *Opuntia macroentra* are actually *O. azurea*.

DESIGN SUGGESTIONS
Mix tuxedo spine with perennials such as canyon penstemon (*Penstemon psuedospectablis*) and buckwheat (*Eriogonum wrightii*). It is small enough to fit in beds 3 feet or wider.

CULTIVATION
Easy to grow and propagate from pads, but more prone to rot than most prickly pears; take care to provide well-drained soil

NOTABLE VARIETIES, FORMS, AND SUBSPECIES
The plant is extremely variable but as it is propagated clonally, most cactus nurseries stock specimens that are compact with desirable long black and white spines.

TUXEDO SPINE PRICKLY PEAR IN FULL BLOOM IN A TUCSON, ARIZONA, GARDEN.

Opuntia santa-rita
(Also sold as *Opuntia violacea var. santa-rita*)

purple prickly pear; Santa Rita prickly pear

Much loved for desert landscaping, its pads turn royal purple or deep red when stressed by drought or cold.

NATIVE HABITAT

Southern Arizona; northeastern Sonora, Mexico

MATURE SIZE

4–6 feet (1.2–1.8 m) tall and 4–5 feet (1.2–1.5 m) wide

HARDINESS

Zone 7

FLOWERING SEASON

Mid- to late spring, depending on location

PURPLE PRICKLY PEAR PUSHING OUT NEW GROWTH IN SPRING.

► Thanks to its pad coloration, *Opuntia santa-rita* is one of the most coveted prickly pears. When its pads are growing in warm, wet weather, they are blue-green tinged with a hint of purple, turning a deep purple in cold or dry weather. Purple prickly pear is a large plant, so care should be taken to site it accordingly. Older plants will form a woody trunk. Purple prickly pear has abundant brown, hairlike glochids, but no spines on most nursery selections.

In the wild, plants have some spines on their upper areoles. Its flowers are a clear yellow that contrasts nicely with the pad color. In cultivation where plants receive occasional irrigation, flowering is often heavy. In late spring, purple prickly pear pushes out new pads, which are sometimes tinged with magenta.

DESIGN SUGGESTIONS

Effective as a large, statuesque plant or focal point in a landscape; also handsome when clustered or mass planted

CULTIVATION

The purple prickly pear is particularly susceptible to cochineal scale (especially in cultivation), which appears as white, cottony dots on the pads. To treat, blast off the scale with a strong jet of water and repeat as necessary.

NOTABLE VARIETIES, FORMS, AND SUBSPECIES

Mountain States Wholesale Nursery in Glendale, Arizona, sells a compact purple prickly pear with fat pads called 'Tubac'.

Peniocereus greggii subsp. *transmontanus*
(Also sold as *Cereus greggii*)

Arizona queen of the night

The outsized and highly fragrant, showy white flowers are much prized—more so than Arizona queen of the night's slender lead-colored stems.

NATIVE HABITAT	MATURE SIZE	HARDINESS	FLOWERING SEASON
The Sonoran Desert below 3300 feet (1000 m) in elevation	Up to 10 feet (3 m) tall and branching as wide as 6 feet (1.8 m)	Zone 8	Late spring to midsummer

► A connoisseur's cactus to be sure, Arizona queen of the night has stems that look a little like burnt sticks. The slender stems emerge from an enormous underground turnip-like tuber that can weigh up to 100 pounds. An interesting feature is that all Arizona queens of the night in an area bloom in synchrony on the same nights, only three to five times per summer. It is one of the rare cactus that typically grow much larger in cultivation than they do in the wild. In habitat, its stems are often eaten by herbivores such as wood rats, and it may only have one or two scraggly stems. It is very hard to find in the wild as it typically grows intertwined with the foliage of shrubs and scrubby desert trees. In gardens where plants are protected from predators, Arizona queen of the night can grow many times larger than in nature. Some gardeners report single plants sporting over 300 flowers. The flowers are typically 3 inches in diameter.

CULINARY VALUE

Native Americans used the roots medicinally and ate them as a vegetable.

DESIGN SUGGESTIONS

Wonderful in a pot trained to a trellis, beneath multi-trunked trees, or intertwining with a chain link or barbwire fence

CULTIVATION

Salvaged tubers are occasionally available from cactus and succulent societies that relocate plants prior to development.

ARIZONA QUEEN OF THE NIGHT INTERLACED WITH THE BRANCHES OF A FOOTHILLS PALO VERDE TREE IN THE AUTHOR'S TUCSON GARDEN.

NOTABLE VARIETIES, FORMS, AND SUBSPECIES

Two subspecies of *Peniocereus greggii* are recognized: *P. greggii* subsp. *transmontanus* and *P. greggii* subsp. *greggii*. The latter has smaller flowers and a greater range in habitat—extending from New Mexico to west Texas and Chihuahua at elevations above 3900 feet (1170 m). Given its range, it should be more cold hardy than *P. greggii* subsp. *transmontanus*.

THE TOTEM POLE'S TOUCHABLE, THORNLESS SKIN MAKES IT AN EXCELLENT CHOICE FOR PLANTING AREAS ADJACENT TO PATHWAYS.

THE FLUTED, BLUE-GREEN COLUMNS OF THE CARDÓN ARE AMONG THE MOST STRIKING OF ALL COLUMNAR SPECIES.

THE SHAGGY TIPS OF SENITA CREATE LIVING SCULPTURE IN A GARDEN.

LUPINE SEEDLINGS SURROUND A YOUNG SAGUARO CACTUS.

▶ The columnar cactus are the largest and most dramatic of all the plants in the cactus family. They are typically much taller than they are wide, without segmented body parts. Some in the group will have single spear-shaped bodies that will eventually sprout arms, while others will have multiple stems emerging from a base in an organ pipe fashion. The group takes in the iconic saguaro cactus (genus *Carnegiea*) as well as specimens such as the Mexican fencepost (genus *Pachycereus*). The columnar structure of these plants recalls Greek architecture. Most have fluted ribs that suggest the Corinthian and Ionic orders. They provide strong vertical elements in a garden.

The one drawback to plants in this group, on the whole, is that they are the least cold-tolerant category. When looking at columnar cactus cold-hardiness numbers, it becomes readily apparent that for the chillier cities in the region, there are few choices that will survive in-ground outside of southern Arizona, California, and parts of New Mexico and west Texas. But as container plants, they can be grown anywhere with winter protection.

SAGUARO CACTUS SET AGAINST A TWO-TONE STUCCO WALL LEND A PLEASING VERTICALITY.

THIS SENITA COMBINES PERFECTLY WITH CREOSOTE BUSH IN THIS NATURALISTIC PHOENIX GARDEN.

NOT ALL CACTUS PLANTINGS HAVE TO BE INFORMAL. IN THIS PLANTING AT SANTA BARBARA'S LOTUSLAND, MEXICAN FENCEPOST CACTUS ADD A FORMAL COLUMNAR TOUCH TO AN ENTRYWAY.

Conspicuous Columnar Cactus

Companion plants for columnar cactus are many. Young columnar cactus enjoy the light shade and frost protection offered by desert trees such as mesquite (*Prosopis* species), palo verde (*Parkinsonia* species), and ironwood (*Olneya tesota*). As plants grow, they look good when grouped next to cactus such as barrels and prickly pears. Also, try pairing columnar plants with red-flowering tough shrubs such as chuperosa (*Justicia californica*) and Baja fairy duster (*Calliandra californica*).

SAGUAROS
GROWING IN
THE FOOTHILLS
OF THE SANTA
CATALINA MOUN-
TAINS NORTH OF
TUCSON.

The most iconic of all cactus, the saguaro is a tall branching column whose anthropomorphic figure has become a mainstay of advertising promoting the Southwest as a tourist destination.

Carnegiea gigantea

saguaro; sahuaro

NATIVE HABITAT

Almost completely restricted to southern and central Arizona, although a few plants jump the Colorado River into California; plentiful in Sonora, Mexico; found growing at elevations between 0 and 4430 feet (0 and 1329 m)

MATURE SIZE

30–52 feet (9–15.6 m) high and eventually branching to 6–8 feet (1.8–2.4 m) across

HARDINESS

Zone 9

FLOWERING SEASON

Mid- to late spring

► Named after the American philanthropist Andrew Carnegie, *Carnegiea gigantea* is the largest cactus in the United States. In the wild, mature specimens can soar to over 52 feet (15.6 m) tall. Mature plants have been known to live for 150 years. The saguaro has pleated ribs that expand and contract during times of wet and dry weather. A large well-hydrated plant can weigh more than 10 tons. Although the saguaro is not listed as endangered or threatened, large-scale urban development in the central Arizona desert has definitely reduced the plant's numbers. To help mitigate habitat destruction, the plant is protected in Arizona by regulations that restrict the harvesting or selling of wild saguaros. For gardeners, seed-grown plants are easily obtained. White- to cream-colored flowers form around the top of the plant when they reach 5 to 8 feet in height. Edible deep-red fruit follows the flowers.

CULINARY VALUE

The deep-red fruit are harvested by several Indian tribes in Arizona and Mexico and eaten fresh or juiced for fermentation into wine.

DESIGN SUGGESTIONS

Truly a formidable sentinel in areas where they can be grown in the ground, saguaros make a bold statement planted in small clusters at the edges of desert tree canopies or against a colored garden wall. In colder climates, they are also easy to grow in pots that can be brought in during winter.

CULTIVATION

If you are transplanting salvaged or bareroot plants, take pains to orient the saguaro the same direction it was in nature or the nursery (for example, south side facing south); if this is unknown, protect the growing tip with shade cloth until it acclimates. Also make sure to plant saguaros at the same level, or slightly higher, than they were growing before. Plants 6 feet tall (1.8 m) or shorter transplant more successfully than larger plants. Because the lateral roots of the saguaro extend many feet out from the center of the plant, care should be taken to locate irrigation emitters well away from the roots to avoid rotting the plant by overwatering.

Cephalocereus senilis

old man of Mexico

The old man of Mexico is a popular cultivated species admired for its white, hairy appearance resembling the Addams Family's "Cousin Itt".

NATIVE HABITAT	MATURE SIZE	HARDINESS	FLOWERING SEASON
Hildalgo and Guanajuato, Mexico	49 feet (15 m) high with stems to 18 inches (45 cm) in diameter	Zone 9b	Midspring

► In habitat, the old man of Mexico can reach a lofty 49 feet (15 m) high and serve as a towering, tree-like specimen. In a garden situation, the old man of Mexico is much smaller and easier to manage in container culture, where it is quite striking. For gardeners north of the border, its use is mostly limited to pots, with the exception of a few warm-winter, largely frost-free cities in the arid West. Its thick, long white hair obscures its body. It only branches basally (from the base), which often leads to plants with an attractive trio of trunks. The shaggy, haywire, hairlike spines of the old man of Mexico are the main draw for gardeners as the plant only produces yellowish-pink flowers on the sides of its stems after it achieves a height of nearly 20 feet (6 m). Collectors have been known to "wash the hair" of the old man of Mexico with diluted detergent to keep the hairlike spines a bright white color.

DESIGN SUGGESTIONS
Old man of Mexico is exceedingly handsome when planted as a pair flanking an entryway, where frost protection is possible. The white spines look especially fetching when planted in brightly glazed pots.

CULTIVATION
Keep this cactus dry in the winter to avoid rotting. Propagate old man of Mexico by stem cuttings in spring. Cut off an arm, let it heal over in the shade for three to five days, and pot in fast-draining soil where it will re-root.

NOTABLE VARIETIES, FORMS, AND SUBSPECIES
A crested form (forma *cristata*) is sometimes found in the trade. It looks like an old man with his white hair parted right down the middle.

A NICELY DISPLAYED SPECIMEN AT CALIFORNIA CACTUS CENTER IN PASADENA.

Myrtillocactus geometrizans

blue flame; bilberry cactus; garambullo; whortleberry cactus

Blue flame boasts a large upright candelabra form with an interesting blue-green color and dark purple, blueberry-sized fruit.

NATIVE HABITAT

Widespread throughout central Mexico from Tamaulipas south to Oaxaca

MATURE SIZE

To 13 feet (3.9 m) tall and 8–12 feet (2.4–3.6 m) wide; crested plants are much smaller. In habitat, some exceptional specimens can reach 30 feet (9 m) high and wide!

HARDINESS

Zone 9b

FLOWERING SEASON

Early spring

▶ In shape, blue flame forms a mass of branches held above a trunk. In the wild, massive blue flame plants often dominate the landscape, forming cactus forests. It stays smaller in cultivation, but can still grow into an impressive specimen in relatively short order. Like many of the larger tree-forming cactus, its cold hardiness (to around 25° F, 4° C) limits the plant to container culture. For containers, the smaller size of the crested form is desirable. The stems of blue flame are 2–4 inches (5.1–10 cm) in diameter. The blue flame cactus begins flowering once it reaches a height of about 2 feet (60 cm).

CULINARY VALUE

Known in Mexico as garambullo, blue flame cactus produces a delicious fruit sold in markets there. The plump, spineless, purple fruit has a sweet taste somewhere between blueberries and cranberries.

DESIGN SUGGESTIONS

The crested form (shown) is an excellent choice staged in a potted cactus collection. In appropriate climates, use the blue flame in the ground as a centerpiece accent plant or at the fringes as a hedge.

CULTIVATION

Cuttings won't root unless temperatures exceed 70° F. To produce fruit, the blue flame needs regular watering over the warm season. To promote the growth of the crest in the crested form, remove any shoots that revert to normal.

NOTABLE VARIETIES, FORMS, AND SUBSPECIES

The crested form, sometimes called dinosaur back, has beautiful crested tops and a beguiling dusty blue color. It makes a great conversation piece as a potted plant on a patio.

THE CRESTED FORM OF THE BLUE FLAME HAS A POWDERY BLUE CAST.

A FULL-SIZED BLUE FLAME CACTUS IN THE MEXICAN STATE OF TAMAULIPAS.

Pachycereus marginatus
(Also sold as *Stenocereus marginatus*)

Mexican fencepost cactus

Mexican fencepost has a strikingly upright form, short spines, and white markings down each rib that lend the plant a pin-striped look.

NATIVE HABITAT	MATURE SIZE	HARDINESS	FLOWERING SEASON
Throughout central Mexico	10–16 feet (3–4.8 m) high with individual stems 3–8 inches (7.6–20 cm) in diameter	Zone 9b	Mid- to late spring

A DOUBLE-LAYERED MEXICAN FENCEPOST FENCE AT THE DESERT BOTANICAL GARDEN, PHOENIX, ARIZONA.

▶ Famously planted around the Mexico City studio of Diego Rivera and Frida Kahlo, and featured in the film *Frida*, the Mexican fencepost is one of the showiest and most garden worthy of the columnar cactus. Its green skin highlights its white rib stripes and its spines are so short as to be nearly inconsequential—easily handled with regular gardening gloves. The white ribs are actually confluent areoles (the tissue that produces spines). Its erect posture is perfect for use as a fence or specimen. Mexican fencepost is either solitary or branching from its base. In Mexico, where it is still widely propagated and used as a living fence, it is often grown in a double layer. Attractive reddish pink flowers form along its ribs, both near its growing tip and down the side of the plant.

DESIGN SUGGESTIONS

Exceedingly desirable against colored walls or as a living fence enclosing a courtyard. Also handsome in containers placed among flowering plants.

CULTIVATION

During the warm season, Mexican fencepost responds well to fairly frequent watering. To propagate as a living fence, cut off tall stems and lay them parallel with the ground in a shallow trench (1–4 inches, 2.5–10 cm deep). Roots will grow from the areoles touching the ground and new stems will pop up from the areoles facing up. Mexican fencepost can be protected from brief periods of frost by placing Styrofoam cups or burlap over its growing tips.

Pachycereus pringlei

cardón

Like the saguaro, cardón is a massive upright plant with pleated ribs. Its beguiling blue-green color and silhouette make it a treasured garden species in warmer climates.

NATIVE HABITAT

Most of the Baja California peninsula, and on the gulf coast of Sonora, Mexico; the northern-most wild plants are found near the town of Caborca in Sonora

MATURE SIZE

20–60 feet (6–18 m) tall (much smaller in cultivation), with stems to 12–24 inches (30–60 cm) in diameter

HARDINESS

Zone 9b

FLOWERING SEASON

Mid- to late spring

THE SPINELESS GROWING TIP OF A MATURE CARDÓN, FOUND IN CENTRAL BAJA CALIFORNIA.

feet in diameter. For such a hulking plant at maturity, cardóns do quite well as container plants and are relatively fast growers. When young, they have white spines on their ridges, but in maturity those spines fall away and are replaced by white-colored felt. Old stems are almost completely spineless. The flowers open after dark and are white, bell-shaped affairs that are pollinated primarily by nectar-feeding bats.

CULINARY VALUE

The Seri Indians eat the pulp (which ranges from red to white) and seeds of the cardón fruit.

DESIGN SUGGESTIONS

Cardón is fantastic as a singular, spear accent plant near the façade of an appropriately scaled home or building, or clustered on a rocky slope.

► Cardón can be easily distinguished from saguaro by its bluish color, more massive stems and, on mature specimens, lower branches than would be found on saguaros. In some sheltered and frost-free locations, cardóns can soar to 60 feet (18 m) high. Their trunks can reach 4 to 5

CULTIVATION

Like many tree-sized cactus, the cardón likes room for its roots to spread out laterally in the soil. A raised bed filled with gritty soil can accomplish this. This giant is readily available in pots as small seed-grown plants.

The senita branches from its base and grows a bearded thatch of spines on its stem tips with maturity. The Spanish vernacular name *senita* or *sinita* roughly translates as little old woman.

Lophocereus schottii
(Also sold as *Pachycereus schottii*)

senita; whisker cactus

NATIVE HABITAT

Senita is found in extreme southern Arizona in Organ Pipe Cactus National Monument, as well as western Sonora, Mexico, and the Baja California peninsula. It will briefly tolerate temperatures to the mid-teens.

MATURE SIZE

10–20 feet (3–6 m) high and 4–10 feet (1.2–3 m) across

HARDINESS

Zone 9

FLOWERING SEASON

Late spring to early summer, with a repeat bloom possible in autumn

▶ The senita branches basally with up to 100 stems. It forms an impressive organ pipe-like arrangement, but the plant is most distinguished by its bristly, beard-like spines that grow into a dense mass at the tips of each stem. White and pink funnel-form flowers open at night and are fragrant. Its juvenile spines are short and stout but the spines that form on the tips of older stems become thick and shaggy. When ripe, the red fruit of the senita is tasty—but unfortunately for human harvesters, it is also highly regarded by birds, which tend to arrive first on the scene. Senita is more cold tolerant than its close relative, the organ pipe cactus. In the wild, senita often grows at the base of ironwood trees (*Olneya tesota*).

CULINARY VALUE

Tasty fruit pursued aggressively by birds

DESIGN SUGGESTIONS

Use senitas in raised planting beds as specimen plants, or in large pots. In cities where in-ground planting is appropriate, senita can serve as a hedge or screening plant.

CULTIVATION

Like several species of columnar cactus, senita is easily propagated from stem cuttings. Cut off an arm, let it heal over in the shade for three days, and pot in fast- draining soil where it will re-root.

NOTABLE VARIETIES, FORMS, AND SUBSPECIES

The most notable form of senita is a thornless cultivated form, totem pole cactus (*Lophocereus schottii* forma *monstrosus*), which is covered in its own entry.

CLOSE-UP OF A SENITA'S WHISKER-LIKE STEM TIP.

SITTING LIKE A SCULPTURE ON A PLINTH, THE SENITA IN THIS GREG CORMAN-DESIGNED TUCSON LANDSCAPE IS WELL SITED.

THE CHARM-
INGLY KNOBBY
STEMS OF TOTEM
POLE ARRANGED
SMARTLY AGAINST
A COLORED WALL
AT B & B CACTUS
FARM IN TUCSON,
ARIZONA.

Totem pole is a knobby lime-green cactus that is exceptionally sculptural and useful in gardens. It is unique among columnar cactus in that it has neither ribs nor spines.

Lophocereus schottii forma *monstrosus*
(Also sold as *Pachycereus schottii*
var. *monstrose* or forma *monstrosus*)

totem pole

NATIVE HABITAT	MATURE SIZE	HARDINESS	FLOWERING SEASON
Baja California, Mexico	To 10 feet high (3 m) and 3–6 feet (0.9–1.8 m) across, although it is usually considerably smaller when grown in containers	Zone 9b	Doesn't flower or set fruit

►Although totem pole's angular stems bear some resemblance to Inuit carved poles, perhaps they better resemble giant, lime-green candles of melted wax. Totem pole is a naturally occurring mutation that is sterile, yet curiously persistent in the wild. It does not flower or set seed; instead surviving because its stems grow new roots when they fall on the ground. All totem poles in the nursery trade have been grown vegetatively—through stem cuttings. It is among the most unusual and interesting of all columnar cactus, and its spineless nature recommends it for many garden applications. It grows as either a single cylinder or more commonly, a plant that branches basally. It is widely grown in the nursery trade and can be used in containers or planted in-ground in appropriate climates. The totem pole's only drawback, like many of the columnar cactus, is its rather wimpy cold hardiness—it will endure brief dips into the low 20s, but only if its stem tips are protected. Placing Styrofoam cups on the growing tips is how the plant is typically protected.

DESIGN SUGGESTIONS

Works well in a sensory garden or children's garden where plants are presented for touching. Totem pole cactus also looks stunning when planted against colored walls or in large entryway pots where appropriate conditions exist.

CULTIVATION

Totem pole is grown from stem cuttings and will only root when temperatures exceed 70° F (21° C).

NOTABLE VARIETIES, FORMS, AND SUBSPECIES

There are two forms of totem pole in the nursery trade: a skinny plant with thinner stems called forma *mieckleyanus*, and the fatter-stemmed and more common plant sold as forma *obesa*.

Erect stems grow up from the bottom of this notable cactus, forming a dense, urn-shaped plant that with maturity does indeed resemble an organ pipe.

Stenocereus thurberi

organ pipe cactus; pitayo dulce

NATIVE HABITAT

Extreme southern Arizona; Sonora, Baja California; Sinaloa, Mexico

MATURE SIZE

To 15–30 feet (4.5–9 m) high, forming clumps as wide; usually smaller in cultivation

HARDINESS

Zone 9b

FLOWERING SEASON

Mid- to late summer

► Organ pipe is a bold plant with handsomely spined stems, very tasty edible fruit, and a pleasing shape. Its spines are reddish when young, turning gray as they mature. Although the organ pipe is sometimes referred to as the Arizona organ pipe, in truth its range barely creeps across the border into the extreme southern part of the state. This restriction is mainly due to the organ pipe's limited cold tolerance—it is the most tender of the Arizona native columnar cactus and temperatures below 25° F (4° C) will kill the growing tips. Double-layered paper bags (such as dog food bags) placed over the growing tips offer additional protection to 10° F (12.2° C), provided the duration of the frost is brief. If tips are damaged, new stems will grow from the point below the damage resulting in a "string of sausages" look. The organ pipe has light pink flowers that open at night and close shortly after sunrise.

CULINARY VALUE

Organ pipe fruit are exceptionally tasty and are harvested annually by the Seri Indians. The Seri refer to them as pitayo dulce and they are reported to have an intense kiwi-strawberry flavor.

DESIGN SUGGESTIONS

Organ pipes can be used as a hedge or as large landscape specimens in raised planters. Like many columnar species, they are also striking in courtyard settings (where adequate space is available) and against courtyard walls.

CULTIVATION

One of the fastest-growing columnar cactus, the organ pipe can put on 1 foot (30 cm) of stem growth per year. In 10 years, a considerably large landscape plant results. It enjoys intense sunlight and will thrive in as much reflected heat and light as you can throw at it.

**THE CONSTRICTED
SAUSAGE-LINK STEMS
OF THIS ORGAN PIPE AT
THE ARIZONA-SONORA
DESERT MUSEUM ARE
THE RESULT OF FROST;
NONETHELESS IT MAKES
A FINE ACCENT IN THIS
COURTYARD GARDEN.**

Cactus Pests

► Although cactus are remarkable for their sturdiness and resilience, they are not without enemies. These invaders come in the form of weevils, beetles, moth larva, mealy bugs, and scale. Controlling these pests can be accomplished by either picking the bugs off by hand (tweezers are helpful) and squishing them (the pressure technique); using a systemic insecticide that gets absorbed in the cactus's tissue, making it toxic to the pest (this is usually a prophylactic measure); or by applying a contact insecticide on the plant that will kill pests. Here are some of the most common pests you might encounter on your cactus specimens:

Blue cactus borer

(Cactobrosis fernaldialis)

This borer, which spends a portion of its life as a moth, is native to the southwestern United States. Its unusual bluish maggot-like larva are about 1/2-inch long at maturity. The larva tunnel though saguaros, barrel cactus (*Ferocactus*) and several species of columnar cactus. The moth larva are particularly nasty in that they are a vector agent (means of transmission) for the *Erwinia* bacteria—a bacteria that rots the interior flesh of the cactus, which is in turn consumed by the larva. The blue cactus borer is most effectively controlled with a systemic insecticide.

Cactus moth

(Cactoblastis cactorum)

The cactus moth was introduced in Australia to reduce populations of unwanted exotic prickly pear cactus. Unfortunately, the moth escaped and was found in the Florida Keys in 1989 and since has made its way to other gulf coast islands. The cactus moth begins life as an orange and black caterpillar that burrows into young, tender prickly pear cactus pads and can eventually kill the mother plant. The USDA has taken aggressive action in an attempt to halt the moth's westward movement. To keep this dreaded pest out of your garden and region, resist the temptation to import cactus pads from Puerto Rico and the Virgin Islands.

Cactus weevil

(Cactophagus spinaloae)

This black weevil with a long, hooked nose resembling an elephant's trunk is about an inch long and looks like a bigger version of his cousin, the agave weevil. The cactus weevil most commonly feeds on Mexican fencepost cactus.

Cochineal scale

(Dactylopius coccus)

Common on prickly pear, this type of scale leaves unsightly white cottony dots on the pads of opuntias. The scale insect itself is filled with a bright red dye that was used in the 18th century as a colorant and is still found in products such as ruby red grapefruit juice as a food coloring. It is best treated by repeatedly spraying off the cottony substance from the pads with a strong jet of water or a solution of water and neem oil. It can be difficult to control but it typically causes only cosmetic damage to the plant.

Giant cactus beetle

(Moneilema gigas)

These large beetles are typically found on cholla and prickly pear cactus but are also common on torch cactus (*Trichocereus* or *Echinopsis*). The adults feed on the apex (tips) of the stems leaving a distinctive half-moon-shaped chew mark on the tip. The female adults lay eggs at the base of the stems, which turn into larva that consume the basal stem, killing it. When the larva pupate, they leave large exit holes. Systemic insecticide is effective but only if applied when the plant is actively growing.

Spine mealy and root mealy bugs

(Pseudococcus subspecies)

These two types of mealy bugs are most often found on varieties of cactus with a dense thatch of spines, such as pincushions (*Mammillaria*). They leave distinctive white pupae on spines and sometimes hide under the lips of pots. Common in cactus collections where plants are grown close together in greenhouses, they can be treated with neem oil (which may require numerous applications), or with a stronger systemic insecticide.

Cactus for Special Purposes

Spineless (or nearly so) and/or friendly to the touch

Astrophytum asterias
Astrophytum myriostigma
Echinocereus carmenensis
Echinocereus knippelianus
Echinocereus rigidissimus
Echinocerus triglochidiatus
   subsp. *mojavensis* forma *inermis*
Lophophora williamsii
Mammillaria plumosa
Mammillaria standleyi
Mammillaria supertexta
Opuntia basilaris
   (no thorns, but has glochids)
Opuntia basilaris × *santa-rita*
   (no thorns, but has glochids)
Opuntia ficus-indica
   (no thorns, but has glochids)
Opuntia fragilis forma denudata
   (no thorns, but has glochids)
Opuntia humifusa
   (small thorns, but has glochids)
Opuntia robusta 'Spineless'
Pachycereus marginatus

Highly scented

Astrophytum capricorne
Echinocactus polycephalus
Echinocereus carmenensis
Echinocereus reichenbachii var. *albispinus*
Escobaria vivipara
Lophocereus schottii
Mammillaria baumii
Mammillaria guelzowiana
Opuntia basilaris
Pediocactus simpsonii
Peniocereus greggii subsp. *transmontanus*

Culinary cactus

Carnegiea gigantea
Cylindropuntia bigelovii
Cylindropuntia echinocarpa
Cylindropuntia imbricata
Cylindropuntia spinosior
Cylindropuntia versicolor
Cylindropuntia whipplei
Echinocereus bonkerae
Echinocereus engelmannii
Echinocereus fendleri
Echinocereus nicholii subsp. *nicholii*
Echinocereus triglochidiatus
   'White Sands Strain'
Echinocerus triglochidiatus
   subsp. *mojavensis* forma *inermis*
Escobaria missouriensis
Escobaria vivipara
Ferocactus cylindraceus
Ferocactus emoryi
Ferocactus herrerae
Ferocactus latispinus
Ferocactus macrodiscus
Ferocactus pilosus
Ferocactus wislizeni
Mammillaria dioica
Mammillaria geminispina
Mammillaria grahamii
Mammillaria guelzowiana
Mammillaria lenta
Myrtillocactus geometrizans
Opuntia engelmannii
Opuntia engelmannii subsp. *lindheimeri*
Opuntia engelmannii subsp. *linguiformis*
Opuntia ficus-indica
Opuntia robusta 'Spineless'
Pachycereus pringlei
Lophocereus schottii
Stenocereus thurberi

Select Retail Cactus Nurseries and Other Resources

United States

Arid Lands Greenhouses
3560 West Bilby Road
Tucson, AZ 85746
520-883-9404

B & B Cactus Farm
11550 East Speedway Boulevard
Tucson, AZ 85748
520-721-4687
www.bandbcactus.com

Bach's Greenhouse Cactus Nursery
8602 North Thornydale Road
Tucson, AZ 86742
520-744-3333
www.bachs-cacti.com

Cistus Nursery
22711 NW Gillihan Road
Sauvie Island, OR 97231
www.cistus.com

Grigsby Cactus Gardens
2326-2354 Bella Vista Drive
Vista, CA 92084-7836
760-727-1323

Landscape Cacti
7711 West Bopp Road
Tucson, AZ 85735
520-883-0020

Mesa Garden (cactus seed)
P.O. Box 72
Belen, NM 87002
www.mesagarden.com

**Miles' To Go Cactus
and Succulent Webalog**
520-682-7272
www.miles2go.com

Plants for the Southwest
50 East Blacklidge Drive
Tucson, AZ 85705
520-628-8773
www.lithops.net

Rio Grande Cacti
2188 NM Highway 1
Socorro, NM 87801
505-835-0687
www.riogrande-cacti.com

Rivenrock Gardens
Organic Edible Cactus
Nipomo, California
www.rivenrock.com

**Santa Fe Greenhouses,
DBA High Country Gardens**
2902 Rufina Street
Santa Fe, NM 87507
800-925-9387
www.highcountrygardens.com

Signature Botanica
P.O. Box 512
Morristown, AZ 85342
623-238-3341
www.signaturebotancia.com

Succulentia
6106 S. 32nd Street
Phoenix, AZ 85042
602-688-4339
www.succulentia.com

Starr Nursery
3340 West Ruthann Road
Tucson, AZ 85745
520-743-7052
www.starr-nursery.com

Sticky Situation
Tucson, AZ
520-743-9761
www.stickysituation.com

Timberline Gardens
11700 West 58th Avenue
Arvada, CO 80002
303-420-4060
www.timberlinegardens.com

Canada

Phoenix Perennials
3380 No. 6 Road
Richmond, BC V6V 1P5
604-270-4133
www.phoenixperennials.com

Southlands Nursery
6550 Balaclava Street
Vancouver, BC V6N 1L9, Canada
604-261-6411
www.southlandsnursery.com

Other cactus resources

Cactus Pruner (tools)
2155 Tabor Drive
Lakewood, Colorado 80215
303-232-8788
www.cactuspruner.com

Rainbow Gardens Bookshop
3620 W. Sahuaro Divide
Tucson, Arizona 85742
866-577-7406
www.rainbowgardensbookshop.com

Plant Hardiness Zones

$$°C = 5/9 × (°F − 32)$$
$$°F = (9/5 × °C) + 32$$

Average Annual Minimum Temperature

ZONE	TEMPERATURE (DEG. F)			TEMPERATURE (DEG. C)		
1	Below		−50	−45.6	and	below
2a	−45	to	−50	−42.8	to	−45.5
2b	−40	to	−45	−40.0	to	−42.7
3a	−35	to	−40	−37.3	to	−40.0
3b	−30	to	−35	−34.5	to	−37.2
4a	−25	to	−30	−31.7	to	−34.4
4b	−20	to	−25	−28.9	to	−31.6
5a	−15	to	−20	−26.2	to	−28.8
5b	−10	to	−15	−23.4	to	−26.1
6a	−5	to	−10	−20.6	to	−23.3
6b	0	to	−5	−17.8	to	−20.5
7a	5	to	0	−15.0	to	−17.7
7b	10	to	5	−12.3	to	−15.0
8a	15	to	10	−9.5	to	−12.2
8b	20	to	15	−6.7	to	−9.4
9a	25	to	20	−3.9	to	−6.6
9b	30	to	25	−1.2	to	−3.8
10a	35	to	30	1.6	to	−1.1
10b	40	to	35	4.4	to	1.7
11	40	and	above	4.5	and	above

To see the U.S. Department of Agriculture Hardiness Zone Map, go to the
U.S. National Arboretum site at http://www.usna.usda.gov/Hardzone/ushzmap.html.

Bibliography

Anderson, Edward F. 2001. *The Cactus Family.* Portland, Oregon: Timber Press.

Anderson, Miles. 2008. *The Complete Illustrated Guide to Growing Cactus and Succulents.* London, England: Lorenz Books.

Blum, W., M. Lange, W. Rischer, and J. Rutow. 1998. *Echinocereus. Fa. Proost N.V.*, Turnhout, Belgium.

Bowers, Rick, Nora Bowers, and Stan Tekiela. 2009. *Cactus of Texas Field Guide.* Cambridge, Minnesota: Adventure Publications.

Ingram, Stephen. 2008. *Cacti, Agaves, and Yuccas of California and Nevada.* Los Olivos, California: Cachuma Press.

Johnson, Matthew Brian. 2004. *Cacti, other Succulents and Unusual Xerophytes of Southern Arizona.* Tucson, Arizona: University of Arizona Press.

Kelaidis, Gwen M. 2007. *Hardy Succulents.* North Adams, Massachusetts: Storey Publishing.

Konings, Ad, and Gertrude Konings. 2009. *Cacti of Texas in their Natural Habitat.* El Paso, Texas: Cichlid Press.

Loflin, Brian, and Shirley Loflin. 2009. *Texas Cacti.* College Station, Texas: Texas A & M University Press.

Mielke, Judy. 1993. *Native Plants for Southwest Landscapes.* Austin, Texas: University of Texas Press.

Niethammer, Carolyn. 2004. *The Prickly Pear Cookbook.* Tucson: Rio Nuevo Publishers.

Phillips, Steven J., and Patricia W. Comus. 2000. *A Natural History of the Sonoran Desert.* Tucson: Arizona-Sonora Desert Museum Press; Berkeley: University of California Press.

Pilbeam, John. 1999. *Mammillaria.* Southampton, U.K.: Cirio Publishing Services Ltd.

Pilbeam, John, and Derek Bowdery, 2005. *Ferocactus.* Norwich, U.K.: British Cactus and Succulent Society.

Preston-Mafham, Ken. 2007. *500 Cacti.* Richmond Hill, Ontario, Canada: Firefly Books Ltd. Publishing.

Preston-Mafham, Ken, and Rod Preston-Mafham. 1991. *Cacti: The Illustrated Dictionary.* Portland, Oregon: Timber Press.

Starr, Greg. 2009. *Cool Plants for Hot Gardens.* Tucson: Rio Nuevo Publishers.

Turner, Raymond M., Janice E. Bowers, Tony L. Burgess. 1995. *Sonoran Desert Plants: An Ecological Atlas.* Tucson: The University of Arizona Press.

Index

About the Author

EDWARD MCCAIN

Scott Calhoun is an award-winning author and garden designer based in Tucson, Arizona. Self-reliant prickly plants, and particularly cactus, have long captured his imagination. In his design practice, he incorporates cactus into every residential space and sees them as the plant family of the future—especially in arid parts of the world.

Scott is the author of six gardening books. His first book, *Yard Full of Sun*, was awarded the 2006 American Horticultural Society Book Award; his second title, *Chasing Wildflowers*, won the Garden Writers Association 2008 Silver Book Award. Scott writes a monthly garden column for *Sunset* magazine and has written for most national gardening magazines. He runs Zona Gardens, a design studio, and gardens, writes, and lectures across the United States. When he is at home, he can often be found in his garden, a magenta glass of prickly pear lemonade in hand and his schnoodle, Macy, at foot. Catch up with Scott at www.zonagardens.com.